LORD GIFFORD AND HIS LECTURES

A Centenary Retrospect

LORD GIFFORD
AND HIS LECTURES

A Centenary Retrospect

STANLEY L. JAKI

Gifford Lecturer, University of Edinburgh
1974-1975 and 1975-1976

1986

SCOTTISH ACADEMIC PRESS

EDINBURGH

MERCER UNIVERSITY PRESS

MACON, GEORGIA

SCOTTISH ACADEMIC PRESS LTD
33 Montgomery Street,
Edinburgh EH7 5JX

ISBN 7073 0465 2

British Library Cataloguing in Publication Data

Jaki, Stanley L.
Lord Gifford and his lectures.
1. Gifford, Adam   2. Natural theology——Biography
3. Theologians——Great Britain——Biography
I. Title
210'.92'4   BL182

ISBN 0-7073-0465-2

Printed in Northern Ireland by The Universities Press (Belfast) Ltd.

Contents

Introduction

The publication of this volume has been prompted by the centenary of a momentous event for modern academic life. Such events are usually marked by pomp and circumstance: display of colourful gowns, tasseled caps, and shining maces, so many medieval paraphernalia. They are jealously kept by modern universities all too ready to forget that a systematic cultivation of natural theology was a principal feature of the medieval intellectual atmosphere which gave rise to universities.

The event in question had a faintly medieval touch by taking place in Granton House, Adam Lord Gifford's antiquarian residence on the northern outskirts of Edinburgh, on the edge of the Firth of Forth. A luscious garden around the house provided the pomp for the signing on August 21, 1885, by Lord Gifford, Associate of Scotland's Court of Session, of his will. A long clause in it offered munificent provisions for the establishment of unofficial lectureships in natural theology at the four Scottish universities. The circumstances of the signing were almost defiantly unpretentious. One of the two witnesses was James Foulis, the Lord Justice's personal physician. The other was John Mackenzie, the doctor's coachman, who hardly ever was farther inside university walls than the spacious Old Court of Edinburgh University, a convenient parking lot then for coaches and horses and now for motorcars.

For some time a victim of steadily debilitating stroke, Lord Gifford undoubtedly had high hopes about the clause of his will relating to the lectureships. He was a man of the highest ideals, driven by steely resolve, and guided by an ample fund of practical sense. Only a fraction of a century was to pass before the Gifford lectures became a byword in the academia far beyond Scotland.

For such an outcome no small credit goes to the

Academic Senates of the four Scottish universities: Edinburgh, Glasgow, Aberdeen, and St. Andrews. Their
archives witness to the care with which they nursed their
respective shares in the munificent endowment and selected
the lecturers who hardly ever failed to be impressed by the
warm and congenial atmosphere provided for them. Yet
those distinguished Senates would have always been the
first to ascribe the lion's share of success to Lord Gifford's
vision. That vision, a Weltanschauung in the best sense,
was as rich in aspects as it was unitary. The richness reveals
itself by a mere look at the titles of his seven lectures
delivered to various audiences between 1872 and 1880, and
published posthumously in 1889. As to unity, it sets the
tone of those parts of his lectures that still deserve reprint-
ing, a circumstance that greatly facilitated the task of
selecting from them the sections reprinted here.

Most of Lord Gifford's lectures have indeed a common
explicit thrust: the indispensability of a well argued natural
knowledge of God for well-being, individual and social. By
the time Lord Gifford delivered his lectures, a classic status
had been achieved by a series of lectures given by John
Henry Newman on the ideals which universities should
emulate. There natural theology was emphatically spoken
of as the backbone of an intellectually coherent and morally
inspiring instructional program of higher education. In all
evidence Lord Gifford formed himself an exalted notion of
natural theology without ever reading Newman's classic.
That notion matured in him in the course of a life spent in
tasks that were hardly philosophical or theological. In his
mind and heart Adam Gifford, as witnessed by his brother's
recollections of him (also reprinted here for the first time
since their first and private publication in 1891), was not so
much a jurist as a philosophical theologian animated by
missionary zeal.

The extent to which the well over a hundred lecturers
carried out their assignment in conformity with Lord
Gifford's specifications is an aim of this essay to evaluate.
Those specifications were not so vague as to make such an
aim questionable. Lord Gifford was liberal enough to invite
outspoken dissent, but it was to be on a specific point:

natural theology, or philosophical discourse about the Ultimate in intelligibility and being. Since a good number of the lecturers came to grip with the assignment specified, the Gifford lectures have grown from a prestigious series into a prominent forum for that officially neglected part of philosophy which is natural theology. A distinct pride of the British Isles, the Gifford lectures seem, after a hundred years, to have assumed a global mission. In a world increasingly bogged down in technological pursuits and at a loss to cope with problems—psychological, social, moral, and ideological—they create, no academic organ has kept so alive some higher perspectives as have the lectureships which Lord Gifford decided to establish a hundred years ago.

A Hundred Years of
GIFFORD LECTURES

The physiognomy, mental no less than physical, of a
country can reveal more readily some of its salient features
to the visitor than to the native. The British owe their first
major portrayal to Voltaire's lengthy visit in London. Yet,
for all his appreciation of the advantageous peculiarities of
British thinking and institutions, Voltaire failed to be struck
by the fact that, unlike Paris, the even greater city of
London was without a university. Had Voltaire taken a
close look at Oxford and Cambridge, he would have found
that, unlike the Sorbonne, the universities of Oxford and
Cambridge existed largely as a charter. The clustering in
both places of individual and fiercely independent colleges
strongly contrasted with the Sorbonne, and even more so
with the stark centralization of the French academic world
which the Revolution imposed on it.

One aspect of British individualism was the facility with
which lectureships could be established by private individuals within university precincts. That Voltaire never
spoke in his *Lettres anglaises* of the Boyle lectureship, which
by the late 1720s had made intellectual history not only in
England but also on the Continent,[1] should seem particularly strange. After all, that lectureship had for its chief aim
the discrediting of atheism, a special concern also for
Voltaire.

The Boyle lectures were the fruit of the insight,
resourcefulness, and commitment of an individual, the

---

1. Especially through the exploitation of Newton's *Principia* on behalf
    of natural theology in *The Confutation of Atheism* (1694) by Richard
    Bentley, the first Boyle lecturer. For details see the Introduction to
    my translation of Kant's *Universal Natural History and Theory of the
    Heavens* (Edinburgh: Scottish Academic Press, 1981), pp. 17 and
    217.

distinguished chemist Robert Boyle, who found ready imitators in England. The most notable of them was John Bampton, canon of Salisbury, whose will provided in 1751 for lectures still given in Oxford by Church of England clergymen every other year, and at times with a reverberation worthy of a strong theological institution.[2] When authors, philosophers, discoverers, and inventors found from the mid-19th century on that public lectures were an effective means of popularity and profit, the endowing of public lectures became a favorite outlet for philanthropists. The number of such lectureships set up in Britain in the closing decades of the 19th century was considerable and some of them quickly became the vehicle of intellectual history such as the Romanes lectures and the Hibbert lectures. Neither of these, to say nothing of similar enterprises, acquired the renown which the Gifford lectures enjoyed almost from their very inception in January 1888.

To begin with, the sum of £80,000 bequeathed by Adam Lord Gifford,[3] associate judge of the Court of Session in Edinburgh, Scotland's highest tribunal, was in itself an extraordinary gesture. Bequests of that size were national news[4] and rightly so if one considers the over 3 million

2. As shown by the reaction to the lectures, *The Limits of Religious Thought* (1858), by H. L. Mansell and *The Incarnation of the Son of God* (1891) by Ch. Gore, a future Gifford lecturer.

3. The most detailed, though not critical, source on Adam Gifford is *Recollections of a Brother, Adam Gifford, One of the Senators of the College of Justice in Scotland under the Title of Lord Gifford*, Printed for the use of the Family by his Brother [John Gifford], 1891, a booklet of 53pp in 12° (with no indication of printer and place). Of its three appendices (the Gifford family tree, the *Scotsman*'s report of Lord Gifford's resignation from the Court of Session and the text of his will establishing the lectureships) only the latter is reprinted in this volume. Lord Gifford's will was entered in the Registry Office of Edinburgh on March 3, 1887. The sections of the will relating to the lectureships were reported in the *Scotsman* on March 10, p. 5, cols. 5–6. Shortly afterwards, (the last two Sundays of March, the 20th and 27th), the will formed the subject of the sermons of the Rev. Charles Volsey, rector of the Theistic Church, near Picadilly, published as Nr. 12 and 13 of vol. X. of *Theistic Sermons*.

4. Thus the *Scotsman* reported (March 4, 1887, p. 3, col. 7) the particulars of the will of George Bentninck, MP from Norfolk, who bequeathed the sum of £72,000.

pounds sterling, or 5 million dollars,[5] which Lord Gifford's munificence would today represent in actual purchasing power. The £8,000, which funded the Hibbert lectures,[6] were a modest amount even with respect to the shares which the Universities of Edinburgh, Glasgow, Aberdeen, and St. Andrews were to have from Lord Gifford's bequest (twenty-five, twenty, twenty, and fifteen thousand pounds respectively). Lord Gifford could hardly doubt that the four universities in question, which received but a few thousand pounds annually at that time from the Public Education Fund,[7] would eagerly accept the terms of his bequest and implement its essentially philosophical objective.

Had Lord Gifford's objective been different he might have left the management of that sum in the hands of a private board of directors, as did the merchant Robert Hibbert. A former student at Emmanuel College, Hibbert might have considered Oxford University, had the latter not been at that time still too much a Church of England stronghold, an anathema for Hibbert, a militant Unitarian. He expected the lectures founded by him to avoid anything—revelation, miracles, and scriptures—that might support dogmatic Christianity in any form. Again, if the lectures were to expound some specific creed, as was the case with the ones founded in Edinburgh in 1872 by the Reverend John Baird, the management of lectureships was best left with a specific church, in that case with the Free Kirk of Scotland. While Lord Gifford expected the lecturers to discuss natural theology with no reference to miracles and revelation, he did not expect the lecturers to inveigh against the supernatural. What he had in mind was a strictly philosophical theology of the Emersonian and Spinozist type and therefore his choice of four universities as the managers of his bequest was particularly apt. The times were also helpful as in the closing decades of the 19th century a very liberal spirit prevailed in the theological

5.   An evaluation provided by the department of economics of Chase Manhattan Bank, through the courtesy of Mr. Hans Ziegler.

6.   See "Hibbert, Robert," in *Dictionary of National Biography*. Another fruit of Hibbert's deed, signed in 1847, two years before his death, was the eventual foundation of the *Hibbert Journal*.

7.   As reported in the *Scotsman*, March 5, 1887, p. 9, col. 7.

faculties of those universities in spite of their manifold ties with Scottish presbyterianism. That Lord Gifford's choice fell on four universities[8] with geographical proximity and common background provided for that healthy competition which is less likely to arise among universities strongly dependent on one higher central administration.

As is well known, Voltaire's most memorable observation about the difference between France and England related to the respective views of space in Cartesian and Newtonian physics. In France space was full, in England it was empty. A perceptive Frenchman going to England around 1887 would have felt he was going from an area full of ideological conflict into an area almost devoid of it. Not that the British Isles had not at times reverberated with conflicts of that type. But they—the emancipation of Catholics and the upsurge of Darwinism—were taken in their stride. The Frenchman in question might have sensed that beneath British pragmatism, so much akin to relativism, there lay perhaps more of that *sens commun* or *bon sens* (of which the French pride themselves)[9] which helps see the difference between truth and the measure (always very meager) of success in convincing one's opponent of it.

Something of that kind of insight seems to be the most overlooked and yet most precious element in the lengthy and careful specifications which Lord Gifford tied to his bequest.[10] This is why, for all his personal persuasions about the convincingness of natural theology when properly articulated, he wanted competition. While he gave sufficient opportunity for each lecturer to present his views, he wanted a great variety of them. Lecturers were to be appointed for a term of two years (each with at least ten

8. The will listed as alternate trustees of the lectureship the Faculty of Advocates (Edinburgh), the Faculty of Surgeons and Physicians in Glasgow, the Faculty of Advocates in Aberdeen, and the Faculty of Physicians and Surgeons in St. Andrews "and of the district twelve miles around it."

9. For details, see my *Uneasy Genius: The Life and Work of Pierre Duhem* (Dordrecht, London, and Boston: Martinus Nijhoff, 1984), pp. 320–23.

10. Several of the early Gifford lectures contain the text of the will relating to the lectureships.

lectures), but no lecturer was to be appointed by any of the four universities for more than three consecutive terms, or six years at most.

Competition was further served by the stipulation that the lecturers were not to be submitted to any religious test. They could be of any denomination, or belong to no church at all. They could even be freethinkers, sceptics, agnostics, provided they were "able reverent men, true thinkers, sincere lovers of and earnest inquirers after truth." The only restriction imposed on them was the duty to discuss natural theology as a science, such as astronomy or chemistry, that is, "without reference to or reliance upon any supposed special exceptional or so-called miraculous revelation." Apart from that they could "freely discuss . . . all questions about man's conceptions of God or the Infinite, their origin, nature, and truth, whether he can have any such conceptions, whether God is under any or what limitations, and so on." The reason for this liberality of mind was Lord Gifford's conviction that "nothing but good can result from free discussion." Such a trust in the process of which the French speak of as "du choc des idées jaillit la vérité" was all the more noteworthy as Lord Gifford firmly believed both in the validity of natural theology and in the relative ease with which it could be communicated. He wanted lectures on the popular level about the loftiest topic, or

> . . . the Knowledge of God, the Infinite, the All, the
> First and Only Cause, the One and the Sole Substance,
> the Sole Being, the Sole Reality, and the Sole
> Existence, the Knowledge of His Nature and
> Attributes, the Knowledge of the Relations which men
> and the whole universe bear to Him, the Knowledge
> of the Nature and Foundation of Ethics or Morals, and
> of all Obligations and Duties thence arising.

Lord Gifford hoped that the lectures would be printed in inexpensive format so that a broad segment of the public might benefit. He certainly did not envisage and much less expect the lectureship to turn into an informal but very informative British philosophical institution. The two elements—one markedly popular, the other deeply

metaphysical or speculative—that set the tone of the bequest
(in addition to its most liberal provisions, both intellectual
and financial), could hardly be given equal justice in the
long run. Lord Gifford might have suspected this had he
been more than an amateur philosopher. For philosophy
was the first love of one who in his early twenties had to
earn his living as clerk in the leather manufacturing business
of his uncle, and from his late twenties on as an advocate.
That he soon became prosperous was due to his excellence
and reliability as a defence lawyer specializing in equity
cases, a field which he preferred because of the role which
common sense and its quick grasp of situations could
effectively play. There was also something of the penetrat-
ing philosopher in Lord Gifford as a judge who was known
to have made up his mind quickly about truth. In its
defence he could be unshakable by any consideration,
though never to the detriment of fairness, as shown by his
often quoted prosecutor's speech in the famed murder trial
of Jessy McIntosh (Mrs. McLachlan).[11]

It was precisely because of his independence of mind
that in spite of his renown as a lawyer he was called rather
late, in 1870, at the age of fifty, to be associate judge of the
Court of Session. Government circles had some uneasiness
about one with the reputation of a populist and ultraliberal.
In the eyes of some he was also a freethinker for his having
ties, tenuous to be sure, only with the Kirk's Free or
anti-establishment branch.[12] As a judge he was in great
demand as a public lecturer whose subjects less frequently
related to jurisprudence than to metaphysics and philosophical religion.[13] From the moment when in 1843 he had heard

11. For the full text, see *Trial of Mrs. McLachlan*, edited by William
 Roughead (Glasgow and Edinburgh: William Hodge and Co.,
 1911), pp. 140–65. Gifford's fairness is acknowledged there on p.
 xliv.

12. Adam Gifford was fourteen when in 1834 Thomas Chalmers began
 his advocacy of the Kirk's freedom from Government supervision,
 and was twenty-three, when the movement formally split the
 Kirk.

13. The small octavo book of 276pp of Lord Gifford's seven published
 lectures does not represent the full contents of his notebooks from
 which they were taken. See pp. 99 and 102.

a series of lectures by Emerson in Edinburgh, Adam Gifford clearly recognized in transcendentalism his own ideology, if not religion. It was not before long that he discovered Spinoza as another hero of his. He, however, never explored his religious and metaphysical ideology to such an extent as to come face to face with the question of whether the God he believed in was a person or not. His conviction about the importance of natural theology ran, however, very deep. He obviously had other motivation than to make appear puny the lectureships that had been established by Baird, Hibbert, and others.[14] The chief aim of his munificence related, as he put it, to the fact that he had been

> for many years deeply and firmly convinced that the true knowledge of God, that is, of the Being, Nature, and Attributes of the Infinite, of the All, of the First and the only Cause, that is, the One and Only Substance and Being, and the true and felt knowledge (not mere nominal knowledge) of the relations of man and of the universe to Him, and of the true foundations of all ethics and morals . . . when really felt and acted on, is the means of man's highest well-being, and the security of his upward progress . . .

Lord Gifford's personal attachment to a philosophical religion was well known in Edinburgh where as a judge, in retirement since 1881 because of growing paralysis, he gave

14. Gifford must have been familiar with the Cunningham lectures, funded by an Edinburgh physician, William B. Webster, in 1862 in memory of the Rev. William Cunningham, a Free Kirk Minister. Also of local provenance was the Croall lectureship established about the same time. More influential than these lectureships in the formation of Gifford's notion of a lectureship may have been the three-year lectureship funded in 1882 by A. J. Balfour, to provide for the discussion of timely subjects in the department of philosophy in the University of Edinburgh. The honor went to a future Gifford lecturer, A. Pringle-Pattison, whose "Balfour philosophical lectures" were printed under the title, *Scottish Philosophy: A Comparison of the Scottish and German Answers to Hume* (1885) and *Hegelianism and Personality* (1887). At that time Pringle-Pattison still used his original family name Seth.

lectures to popular audiences on such lofty subjects as Emerson, substance, Hindu incarnationism, and St. Bernard. The latter, regardless of his having been a monk and a medieval at that, appealed to him as the noblest realization of a single-minded devotion to the highest ideals. All this became widely known beyond Edinburgh when James H. Stirling, the first to serve there as Gifford lecturer, devoted in January 1889 the first of his second series of lectures to a collection of Lord Gifford's lectures that had just been printed privately for family and friends.

In several aspects, except one, Stirling typified many of the future Gifford lecturers, a total of about hundred-fifty so far. Only a handful of them, (Balfour, Haldane, Dawson, were, for instance, like Stirling, non-academics). Stirling, a native of Edinburgh, certainly set the pattern insofar as reliance on native talent was concerned. Almost a third of Gifford lecturers were Scots, or teachers at one time or another at the four Scottish universities. (The appointment of the Anglican bishop of Durham, Henson, had something to do with his Scottish wife's numerous ties north of the Border). Not unexpectedly, over two thirds of the lecturers were from Great Britain, with Oxford and Cambridge contributing over thirty lecturers each. The need to lecture in English had offset the disadvantage which Americans may have had owing to their distance from the scene. Against the fourteen Americans, France and Germany were represented by only six each. Three came from Holland, four from Switzerland, one from Sweden, Denmark, Italy, and Finland. That the delivery of the lectures in French became acceptable (Boutroux, Bidez, Bergson, Gilson and Marcel availed themselves of that privilege) showed something of the fact that contrary to the founder's express wish, the lectures were not to be a popular fare. When, however, the message was highly controversial, such as Barth's excoriation of natural theology, delivery in foreign tongue provided at least an exotic touch.

Stirling anticipated a slight bent on popularity with humorous or provocative asides. The closeness, conceptual and historical, of natural theology to credal theologies was as much an opportunity for a gentle lampooning of ecclesiastics, old and new, as was the freedom claimed by philosophical discourse on any subject, be it the loftiest. The frequent interpolations, (applause) or (laughter), in the detailed accounts of each of Stirling's lectures in the *Scotsman*,[15] Edinburgh's leading daily, showed that even those who could not really follow the soaring thought befitting an advocate of German idealism, were not altogether disappointed. It did not, however, become necessary for Stirling to make good his promise that he would deliver each one of the lectures again, because at first the great Natural History Lecture Hall was too small to accommodate all those requesting admission.[16]

What happened in Stirling's case repeated itself many times in subsequent years. If a Gifford lecturer drew an average audience of about fifty, he had to congratulate himself. Such was at least the view of Samuel Alexander whose first lecture was attended by several hundred, a number that quickly dropped to about fifty.[17] Others, even some luminaries, drew on the average a mere dozen or even less, and this could happen even to a celebrity like Niels Bohr. Soon he was written off as the "boring Bohr" by science students, all eager at first to attend. One of them recalled from a distance of almost forty years only Bohr's endless references to "the box," the central piece of Bohr's thought-experiment aimed at showing the impossibility of contravening Heisenberg's uncertainty principle.

Whether a good speaker or not, the Gifford lecturer was not to become a popular lecturer, and for two reasons. One was his subject matter—hardly as much within the ken of the broader public as Lord Gifford imagined. The other was his usually eminent academic standing which is reached by qualifications other than the skill to hold audiences spellbound. In fact, the four committees in charge of selecting the Gifford lecturer vied with one another from the very start

15.   In the Monday issues between January 14 and April 8 and with an average length of a thousand words.
16.   *Scotsman*, Jan. 11, 1887, p. 4, col. 6.
17.   See *Philosophical and Literary Pieces by Samuel Alexander*, edited, with a memoir, by his literary executor, J. L. [John Laird] (London: Macmillan and Co., 1939), pp. 60–61.

to secure prominent academic figures. The Gifford commit-
tee of the University of St Andrews advertised, in 1888, for
candidates, but did not repeat a procedure which encour-
aged less than second-rate thinkers to offer their good
services.[18] A major lure for them was, of course, the
stipend, about £400 for one series of lectures, which was
representative of the sum offered by the three other Gifford
committees. The sum was almost twice the yearly salary of
a professor and the minimum income needed through late
Victorian times to maintain middle-class life standard. No
wonder that Pfleiderer, the third Gifford lecturer in Edinburgh, made the comment still remembered there: "Die
Ehre ist nicht gross, aber der Gehalt ist kolossal" ("The
honor is not great but the honorarium is colossal"). Soon
the honor was as great as the honorarium which stood at
about £600 per year in the 1930s.[19] Following the weaken-
ing of the pound, to say nothing of runaway inflation in the
post-World-War-II period, the honor began to outstrip the
honorarium which now stands at about £1,200 per year, a
sum not exceeding the honorarium given for a single lecture
to major guest lecturers at American universities. In the late
1960s Sir Malcolm Knox merely reported a widely shared
view when he stated in the Introduction to his Gifford
lectures: "A few years ago, when I introduced a Gifford
lecturer [O. Chadwick] to a St. Andrews audience, I said
that appointment to a Gifford lectureship was one of the
two highest honors which a scholar could receive."[20] The
other in question seemed to be a Nobel Prize.

In imparting such an esteem to the Gifford lectureship,
the first important single factor was the publication of
William James' *The Varieties of Religious Experience: A Study
in Human Nature*, which for all its size became a runaway

18.   Of the ten candidates only five had respectable academic positions.
19.   In addition to lodgings at the Royal Institution, Faraday drew as its
       director an annual stipend of £200. For further details, see H. Rose
       and S. Rose, *Science and Society* (Harmondsworth: Penguin Books,
       1969), p. 33. For a published figure relating to the early 1930s, see
       Laurence K. Shook, *Etienne Gilson* (Toronto: Pontifical Institute of
       Mediaeval Studies, 1984), p. 183, where the sum £550 is given for
       one series of lectures.
20.   Sir Malcolm Knox, *Action*, Preface.

bestseller following its first printing in June 1902. Six years later it was in its fifteenth impression with all its copies informing countless readers on the title page that the book was the text of "The Gifford Lectures on Natural Religion delivered at Edinburgh in 1901–1902." Whatever one's disagreement with James' trend of thought which, as he clearly admitted in the concluding chapter, led, if taken with philosophical rigor, to polytheism, the wealth of material and the enchanting form of its presentation could only develop the renown of the lectureship itself. Moreover, did it not enhance the lectureship, if it was true that, as James stated at the outset, the book in question would not have been written but for the invitation to serve as Gifford lecturer? James' masterpiece was not the only such work that owed its very birth to the challenge of a Gifford lectureship.[21]

Great books represent a great profit for philosophy at least in the sense that they amply reveal their author's philosophical preoccupations, preferences, and premises. In that sense James was certainly a great philosopher. Not only was he unafraid to spell out polytheism as the inevitable end-stage of his religious philosophy, but, subsequent to his lectures, he also advocated, and logically so, a sort of polycosmism, to characterize succinctly his doctrine of a pluralistic universe. This fragmentation of the universe, so dear for the purposes of James, who viewed as the chief enemy that very Catholicism which held fast to the doctrine of creation out of nothing[22] (the only sound basis of a

21.   Similar admission was made by Alexander and Sherrington.
22.   "I doubt whether the earth supports a more genuine enemy of all that the Catholic Church *inwardly* stands for than I do—*écrasez l'infame* is the only way I can feel about it," wrote James to Mrs. Henry Whitman (see *The Letters of William James*, vol. ii, pp. 126–27), in a letter also printed in *The Philosophy of William James: Selected from His Chief Works*, with an introduction by Horace M. Kallen (New York: The Modern Library, n.d.), pp. 309–10. In *The Pluralistic Universe* James denounced the doctrine of creation out of nothing as one which "has not sweep and infinity enough to meet the requirements of even the illiterate natives of India" (p. 29). This work was the text of James' Hibbert lectures, given in 1909 in Manchester College, Oxford.

universe worthy of the name), is a philosophically most instructive process. It is precisely by its very shock that such a process may awaken the unwary and gratify cultivators of a traditional natural theology. Their number was never great in modern times and was largely limited to traditional Catholic intellectual circles, around 1900 no less than now.

Typically, the protest against a natural theology which does not include the reason's ability to infer the existence of a personal Creator, came from Catholics following Müller's first course in Glasgow. The immediate point at issue was Müller's inveighing against miracles, and in particular against what he called Catholic miracle-mongering, on the ground that in a scientific treatment of religious data no fact can be considered miraculous. Such was not a scientific precept but a pseudo-philosophical one, systematically slighting certain facts, of which Müller remained unaware. He even failed to see the irony when in replying to those critics he claimed that he had not intended to cast doubt on the miracle of Christ.[23] Yet, in his third course, he extolled Jesus as the prophet who wanted faith in Him with no reliance on miracles.[24]

The problem of miracles was only a part of the most problematic aspect of the entire history of the Gifford lectures. Miracles were claimed only within the Christian context imposing a thorough attention to the demands of reason. That context was of necessity a tradition adverse to liberalism and modernism. What was true about miracles, was also true of natural theology insofar as it implied the strict demonstrability of the existence of a personal Creator. That demonstrability alone bars the possibility that religion should turn, however subtly, into man's worshipping nature and himself. Spinozism, Hegelianism, spiritual monism, and transcendental evolutionism are so many cases in point. The problem, as will be seen, became crystallized in the notion of Christian philosophy, a notion of central

23.   Müller, *Anthropological Religion*, p. vi.
24.   Ibid., pp. xix–xx.

relevance for the evaluation of the Gifford lectures.[25] However, Gifford lectures had been given for almost half a century before that problem received a memorable articulation and by one who also served as a Gifford lecturer.

Thus from the very start the lecturers chosen mostly represented the prevailing philosophical fashions hardly germane to the concern whether the cause of natural theology would truly be served. The lecturers in turn did not always feel an obligation to go beyond their specific interests to the ultimate foundations of existence and morality. This trend was quickly set, although in addition to Müller two others, Lang and Tylor, of the first four Gifford lecturers had religious anthropology as their specialty. A perusal of their lectures might have justified the obvious though superficial conclusion that nothing could reasonably be inferred about a personal God's existence. Tylor took to the shallows of empiricism and relativism. His lectures (never published) were long remembered in St. Andrews for his display of exotic items of witchcraft and similar paraphernalia which he, as keeper of the University Museum of Oxford, had at his ready disposal.[26] Lang, a former academic and widely read author, insisted that the animism of savage peoples was a deterioration of a primitive and pure religion. But to this implicitly metaphysical point he provided no epistemological basis. As to Müller, he found true belief in God whether he surveyed nature

25. A brief but telling intimation of that problem is noticeable in the first of those evaluations, *Recent Theistic Discussions: The Twentieth Series of Croall Lectures* (Edinburgh: T. &. T. Clark, 1921), by William L. Davidson, Professor of Logic and Metaphysics in the University of Aberdeen. It was with a reference to the Westminster Catechism that he broached (p. 25) the inadequacy of a natural theology ambiguous about the personal God, Creator and Lawgiver. For reasons that will be discussed later, the question of Christian philosophy is central in the unpublished doctoral dissertation (University of Leeds, May 1966), "The Concept of Natural Theology in the Gifford Lectures" (536 typewritten pp) by Bernard E. Jones, Lamplough professor of theology in Wesley College, Bristol. See also note 44 below.

26. As reported by Davidson, *op. cit.*, p. 175.

worship, ancestor worship, ethical myths, and primitive rites intimating belief in immortality. That he never took pains to give a definition of God or to outline his epistemology, could but dismay even those readers of his who did not suspect that the famed editor-translator of numerous sacred books of the East was rather cavalier with his interpretation of texts and of factual data. He was not even reluctant to present Cardinal Newman as an opponent of miracles, although the latter merely spoke against credulity about them.[27]

Such pitfalls could be readily avoided by using the Gifford lectureship as a platform to present, with no interpretation whatever, the factual data of one's researches in some specific area of studies dealing with religion. A case in point was Marett's lectures on primitive peoples' sacramentology. The most massive example of such a circumventing of the Founder's aims was the two thick volumes which Sir James Frazer presented on the beliefs of aborigines. No less frustrating could be Lanciani's lectures to anyone who desired to hear, however little, about natural theology. Almost as void of that subject was the volume containing Ramsay's lectures. Perhaps this was fortunate. For when a tireless excavator like Sayce was tempted by the opportunities of the lectureship to become a theoretician of comparative religion, the lack of qualification for such a role became immediately obvious. In 1903 no longer could a serious scholar claim, without appearing a cheap popularizer, that the Christian dogma of Trinity was derived from the cosmogony of Heliopolis.

The discussion of early Greek or Roman religion was a problematic ground for more than one reason. The measure of purity which one was willing to attribute to ancient Greek theism was, on the one hand, a testing ground for natural theology, but, on the other hand, it could also raise searching questions about the impact which Christian revelation made on natural theology. Adam was rather reluctant to involve himself in such questions. Campbell was, however, willing to the point of claiming that if

27.   Müller, *Anthropological Religion*, pp. vi–viii.

Christianity was true then Hellenic religion too was in part true. He did not face up to the reverse of the question: What if Christian religion was false? After all, he claimed it to be deficient in some aspects such as the promotion of self-culture and of political duty. No such perplexities transpired from Fowler's meticulous account of Roman religion where the portrayal of Stoic beliefs marks the scholarly high point.

With respect to ancient Greek religion Edward Caird, Master of Balliol, put himself at the other end of the spectrum by being thoroughly interpretative. Needless to say, the interpreter was Hegel as befitted one whose older brother, John Caird, had earned fame for himself as one who "preached Hegelianism from the pulpit"[28] before becoming Principal of Glasgow University. John Caird was the first of those who stretched the stated limits of the lectureship to accommodate an apologetic of Christian theism. Of course, the Christianity that could be defended in Hegelian terms was hardly identical with itself. Hegelianizing divines had little use, then or later, for the warning of McTaggart, the foremost expert in the 1890s on Hegel and a firm atheist to boot, that as far as theism, let alone Christian theism, was concerned, Hegel was "an enemy in disguise, the least evident and the most dangerous."[29]

The disguise could not have been more alluring as it exuded a missionary zeal. Its fountainhead was T. H. Green whose basic contention that the real consisted in relations could be maintained with no reference to Hegel. The ultimate unfolding of that contention that the entire universe of existents was a construction of the mind became transparently Hegelian when it came to the relation-making process. For it was only by a reliance on Hegelian dialectic that the mind's growth into the eternal consciousness could include all the relations involved in the stages of Darwinian

28. See F. Copleston, *A History of Philosophy*. *Volume 8. Modern Philosophy: Bentham to Russell. Part I. British Empiricism and the Idealist Movement in Great Britain* (Garden City NY: Doubleday Image Books, 1967), p. 209.
29. J. M. E. McTaggart, *Studies in Hegelian Cosmology* (Cambridge: University Press, 1901), p. 250.

evolutionism. Such a vision could readily spark a liberal evangelism which Green's many students enthusiastically advocated in their at times very distinguished public careers, which included prominent professorships of philosophy. In that group belonged most contributors to the collection, *Essays in Philosophical Criticism*, published in 1883 in honor of Green who died a year earlier.[30] Of the nine contributors, none beyond their late twenties or early thirties, five—Seth (Pringle-Pattison), J. B. Haldane, Bosanquet, Sorley, and Jones—were to become Gifford lecturers.

By then the program of Green and of his outspokenly Hegelian successor, W. Wallace (an early Gifford lecturer himself, who in his Gifford lectures presented Christ in an unmistakably Hegelian fashion as a *natural* theologian hostile to miracles), had to be articulated against Bradleian absolutism in which no logical room could be made for a personal Absolute. Such is the reason for the personalist idealism which is the backbone of the natural theologies set forth by those five and also by Ward and Webb. Tellingly, even Pringle-Pattison (Seth), who in his Aberdeen lectures tried, as much as an idealist could, to graft personality on the Absolute, almost came to agree with Bradley in his Edinburgh lectures a decade later. As to Bosanquet, who claimed that "we experience the Absolute better than we experience anything else,"[31] he became so much taken up with the "anything else," or sundry concrete data, as to sound time and again as a materialist. (Idealism was once more a phase of the not-so-ideal oscillation from one extreme to the other.) For all his advocacy of personalism Bosanquet's discourse was a far cry from that strictly personalist theism which Christian theological tradition wanted to be the capping stone of philosophical discourse about the Ultimate or Absolute.

The irony of that contrast had to be glaring to any reader of Haldane's lectures which began with a reference to

---

30.   Edited by A. Seth (Pringle-Pattison) and R. B. Haldane (London: Longmans, Green and Co., 1983), 277pp.
31.   Bosanquet, *The Principle of Individuality and Value*, p. 27.

Newman's advocacy of a science of God in *The Idea of a University*. Haldane's was a very rare reference by Gifford lecturers to a book which contains a passionate and elaborate plea on behalf of the central role to be given to the classic proofs of the existence of God in higher education.[32] Haldane seemed to overlook the fact that in spite of its non-Thomist style, Newman's natural theology made no room for an obliteration of God's personality in the Absolute Mind of Hegel whose disciple Haldane wanted to be remembered. The personality of the Absolute was no less ambiguous in the lectures of Watson who ended with an encomium of Hegel's Absolute Spirit. As to Laurie's idealism it hardly allowed for a real God in spite of Laurie's occasional assertion of ordinary reality in the style of Scottish common sense philosophers.

It is not entirely speculative to suppose that had Robert Flint not died before he could write and deliver his lectures, a broadside might have been fired at the Hegelianization of natural theology by means of Gifford lectures. A generation earlier, at the height of his career, Flint made a name for himself by his *Theism*, a series of Baird lectures, and, no less importantly, by a history of modern European thought of which the *Examiner* declared: "It is quite refreshing to see the Hegelian doctrines so fearlessly analysed, and its difficulties and deficiencies so clearly exposed to the ordinary understanding as is here done."[33] Unlike Flint, Henry Jones had the good fortune of writing and delivering his lectures just before he died. As an idealist who tried to reach God mainly through considerations of moral values, he had to fall back ultimately on a Kantian endorsement of the primacy of faith. In his idealist perspective ontological contingency was much less than the basic attribute of the entire realm of finite existents. The realm of moral values

---

32.   See especially pp. 26, 61 and 69 in *The Idea of a University Defined and Illustrated* (London: Longmans, Green and Co., 1888), and especially the distinction there between natural theology and a mere "physical" theology.

33.   Passage reprinted in the page preceding the title page of Flint's *Theism* (Edinburgh: William Blackwood and Sons, 1877).

was also the basis for the lectures of Sorley, an advocate of personal idealism.

Of course, once personality was ascribed to God, He was, as is one person in regard to another, though in an immensely higher sense, set apart and therefore His transcendence could naturally be spoken of as revealing a truly creative power with respect to other beings. Most importantly, such a God could be worshipped in the strict sense, another special requisite made by Christian theological tradition to natural theology. Needless to say, the idea of an Absolute to be worshipped could not emerge within the absolutist idealism of Josiah Royce. In fact its end-point was the absolutization of man, "a freeman who owned no less the world than the Absolute did." About such a God one could quip, as William James teased Royce, a colleague of his at Harvard: "Josh, the Absolute must have fun being made of you."[34] No less teasing, if not farcical, was the opposite extreme, the surrender to an ennobled form of polytheism, which James unabashedly spelled out as the logical result of his interpretation of the varieties of religious experience. It was another matter, whether James did justice to all the varieties of that experience by claiming that all of them—from an entranced sorcery to the lucidity of Saint Theresa's accounts—were the fruit of the same psychological urge. It was still another matter whether one could live in a world which was the juxtaposed sum of as many worlds as there were personal experiences. Such a world was inconsistent and incoherent to the degree that it could not be created by a rational Creator, a conclusion which James certainly relished and perhaps wanted above all to appear plausible.

The reason or the inspiration behind this option of James was an elemental wish to let the will have the freedom to find its fulfillment in the faith most appropriate to its strivings.[35] The intellectual justification of this was in

34.   Personal communication from V. Buranelli, author of *Josiah Royce* (New York: Twayne Publishers, 1964).
35.   The very gist of James' essay, "The Will to Believe" (1895), which for all of James' good intentions rightly aroused the suspicion that its argument provided justification for any course of action.

James' view that neither empiricism nor determinism were self-containing. This meant that science too rested on non-scientific considerations which were quickly labeled as various faiths or fiducial stances. The exploitation of this view on behalf of theism was most memorably done by Balfour in two series of Gifford lectures, further articulations of his much earlier work, *Defence of Philosophical Doubt, being an Essay on the Foundations of Belief*. It was that book which provided an earlier Gifford lecturer, Fraser, with his philosophy of theism.

The provenance of philosophical faith on which Pfleiderer's lectures were based had for its source the Kantian precept that reason had to be curtailed in order to make room for faith. Such a reliance on Kant was part of misconception, intensely cultivated about him by Neo-Kantians. They systematically overlooked Kant's admiration for Rousseau's anthropological program, a definitive emancipation of man from all religion if it meant a God who could both create and reveal.[36] Bruce, another Protestant divine among the early Gifford lecturers, showed far greater care in safeguarding the basic dogmas of Christianity from being diluted in idealism. In fact he urged that a philosophical theism has to provide a reasonable defence of the existence not only of a God but of a providential God. To be sure, he did not claim to offer an "absolutely demonstrative reasoning." The phrase was significant for reasons that will be discussed later. Quite the opposite was the moral of the lectures by the church historian Gwatkin, who advocated as theism what he called a "broad church" creed, that is, a high minded commitment to brotherly love.

Religion conceived in such a way was hardly distinguishable from an immanentist humanism. This could be the result not only of a discourse which did not claim to be systematic and rigorous, but also when the opposite was true as with Samuel Alexander's lectures. They were acclaimed as the "boldest adventure in detailed speculative

36.   For details and documentation see my *Angels, Apes and Men* (La Salle ILL Sherwood Sugden, 1983), pp. 27–29 and 42–44.

metaphysics" attempted since Hobbes by any English writer.[37] His professed aim was a thorough realism which he worked out by starting with space-time, though not under the influence of Einstein who about the same time worked out a space-time very different from a realist or common sense perception of it. But Alexander's leading idea was less a common sense judgment than a self-creating tendency which made his space-time unfold itself through successive gradations from the simplest to the most developed entities. Among the latter were not only the human mind but also the actual God whom Alexander described as "the ideal God in embryo" or the still unfolding space-time.[38] The result was a dynamically recast Spinozism which could but delight Alexander. He expressed supreme satisfaction in the possibility that of his achievement nothing more would be said than that he "had erred with Spinoza."

Alexander clearly perceived that should the immortality of man's self-conscious soul be "verified," his system "would have to be seriously modified or abandoned."[39] Much the same holds true of Whitehead's process philosophy, which allows only an imperfect God and a very imperfect mortal soul, and of Morgan's emergent evolutionism. Had Driesch been more perspicacious, he might have perceived that the vitalism he pleaded for as a biologist was in fact an idealized all-pervading *nisus* which was later articulated with philosophical originality by Alexander, Whitehead, and Morgan, and without it by J. S. Haldane. In the latter's old-fashioned idealism the mechanistic reductionism was merely exchanged by a super-reductionism in which space-time was declared to be the ultimate entity. Another biologist, Thomson, avoided philosophy in his

37.   A statement of J. Laird in *Philosophical and Literary Pieces by Samuel Alexander*, p. 61.

38.   Alexander, *Space, Time and Deity*, vol. 2, p. 365. Clearly, a soul so different from the material body as to survive its dissolution, represents a radical break in the cosmic unfolding as understood by Alexander and implicitly destroys the view that the "distinctive character of deity is not creative but created" (ibid., p. 397).

39.   Ibid., p. 424.

emphasis on the inadequacy of exclusively mechanistic laws in biological research. Particularly effective was that approach in the investigation of the mind-body problem by Sherrington who reserved for a later time his categorical endorsement of dualism as being equivalent to belief in the individual soul's immortality.[40]

The fundamental and all-purpose role assigned to *nisus* illustrated the essentially philosophical character of the idea of evolution as distinguished from any of its mechanism, such as natural selection, a strictly scientific proposition. This distinction was much emphasized by Stokes, who for many years was the only physicist to deliver Gifford lectures. (Lord Kelvin, whose appointment was repeatedly urged by Tait in Edinburgh, was never invited). Stokes was a latter-day Paley who set great store by the design argument, especially through a memorable analysis of the optics embodied in the structure of the eye. Apart from that he unabashedly submitted traditional arguments, and declared already in his first lecture that the free human will demanded for its explanation a personal God with complete freedom. The approach of Hobson, the second physicist to give Gifford lectures, could not have been more different. His emphasis was on showing, in a manner harking back to Poincaré, the conceptual limits and high revisability of "laws" established by physicists. He wanted to secure thereby a "perfect freedom of Religious and Philosophical thought from any fear of destructive inference from the side of Natural Science," provided that neither theology nor philosophy encroached on the domain of natural sciences. That the aim of his twenty lectures was not "to indicate the

40.   It is stated in *Sherrington: His Life and Thought* by John C. Eccles and William C. Gibson (Berlin: Springer International, 1979, p. 155) that Sherrington came to regret that because of his critics he had eliminated the distinctly religious passages from the second and shortened version (1952) of *Man on his Nature* which saw a widespread circulation through paperback editions. Nine days before his death Sherrington disclosed to Eccles: "For me now the only reality is the human soul." Quoted in J. C. Eccles, *Facing Reality* (New York: Springer Verlag, 1970), p. 174.

use which Religious and Philosophical thought may make of this freedom,"[41] was true enough.

Hobson was not the first or the last to take such liberty with the stated aim of the lectureship. The next major example was Eddington, the third physicist to give Gifford lectures, who preferred to remain silent about God. While Eddington's idealist interpretation of modern physics could appear an effective demolition of materialism, its real outcome, solipsism, openly admitted by Eddington several years earlier, was hardly to benefit the cause of theism. As to Eddington's defense of free will with a reliance on Heisenberg's uncertainty principle, it was an effort which even to Eddington himself had to appear, within a few years, as rather nonsensical.[42] The God which emerged from the interpretation of modern physics by the Anglican bishop W. Barnes, a mathematical physicist by first training, could make but uneasy those constituting the High Church.

To some extent this was also true of Gifford lectures by other Church of England dignitaries. One wonders whether any comfort may have been derived by the British Tommy in the trenches of Flanders from reading Inge's lectures, a vast monograph on Plotinus. A non-Christian philosopher on crucial points even according to Inge's admission, Plotinus was Inge's chief solace during the trials of World War I of which he saw nothing at close range. As to Temple, Henson, and Gore, in one way or another they echoed a Kantian scepticism with respect to metaphysics as a backbone of natural theology. The latter became in their hands a mere possibility or at most a probability. Even less was the claim of the Swedish Lutheran Archbishop, Söderblom, who saw in all religions an evidence of a revelation which precisely because of this could not be a

41. Hobson, *The Domain of Natural Science*, p. 499. Much the same theme was elaborated, though with far fewer references to science, in Boutroux's lectures.

42. Eddington, *The Philosophy of Physical Science* (London: Macmillan, 1939), p. 182. For further details, see my article, "Chance or Reality: Interactions in Nature versus Measurements in Physics," *Philosophia* (Athens) 10–11 (1980–81): 85–102.

revelation properly so-called. But once the status of God who could reveal himself in a special way was called into doubt, however indirectly, the status of God who manifests himself through the natural realm also became doubtful. The position of these churchmen was the kind of theological liberalism for which revelation was a distinct burden. The foremost critic of that position was, of course, Karl Barth who by the logic of his animated defence of revelation was driven into a no less animated hostility toward any natural knowledge of God. He was in fact most reluctant to accept the invitation to serve as a Gifford lecturer until given the assurance that Lord Gifford's stipulations were liberal enough to accommodate even a sustained attack on natural theology.

Barth's hostility to natural theology which, as he knew all too well, had far more respectable versions than the one construed within the context of 18th-century deistic optimism, was consistent enough to become a sustained hostility to philosophy. In fact, no other prominent Christian theologian frowned on philosophy so much as Barth did. His Gifford lectures were an animated commentary on the Scottish Confession of 1560, although they could have become a major presentation of his chief contention that biblical revelation was a rebuttal and rejection of natural theology. The opportunity lost thereby was all the greater because Barth himself found it important to answer lecture by lecture a series of four lectures given by Gilson before the Protestant Faculty of theology in Paris in 1933 on the nature of theology as a "fides quaerens intellectum," published as *Christianisme et philosophie*.

Gilson, the first Catholic Gifford lecturer,[43] did not seize the opportunity provided by the lectures to set forth a systematic natural theology in which he had considerable interest. To be sure, *The Spirit of Medieval Philosophy* was not without some pages suggestive of a system. But the book was above all a presentation of a phase of the history

43.   Not counting, of course, Baron von Hügel, who was forced by ill health to resign his lectureship for 1924–26 in Edinburgh. His posthumously published *The Reality of God* (1931) contains some of the material he meant to include in the lectures.

of philosophy by one who always considered himself a historian of philosophy and who showed real concern only about such criticism of that book which claimed it to be a philosophy, indeed an apologetic in disguise, and not a history. Yet, Gilson was an outstanding historian of philosophy only because he had unusual philosophical discernment. Otherwise he would not have perceived, already as a doctoral student untrained in scholastic philosophy, that Descartes had systematically misrepresented pivotal scholastic terms. In fact, Gilson had the insight of laying bare, just before his delivery of the lectures, potentially most serious chinks in some resplendent neo-scholastic armor that bespoke of the intrusion of Kantianism largely through the preconceptions of Maréchal and his followers. Such a chink was inflicted, Gilson noted, on a later edition of a work by one of neo-scholasticism's founder, Cardinal Mercier, who on account of the enormous demands on his time and energy had to entrust the task to someone else. For the same reason the Cardinal could not accept after World War I the invitation of St. Andrews to serve as a Gifford lecturer.

One can only speculate as to the benefit for natural theology had Gilson used his Gifford lectures for a systematic presentation of his epistemology, an epistemology rooted in what he called "Christian philosophy."[44] The

44. For an excellent summary of that notion, the disputes it stirred among Thomists, and some Protestant reaction to it, see L. K. Shook, *Gilson*, pp. 198–204. While acknowledging the importance of Gilson's notion of Christian philosophy, Jones, in his doctoral dissertation (see note 25 above), ignored its consequences in two ways. First, he took it for just another point of view, however enlightening. Thus his appraisal of the Gifford lectures amounted to the claim that according to the "earnest enquirers" (Gifford lecturers) God's existence could only be argued as a "probable" truth, a result which Jones took for the only philosophical requirement for the construction of a Christian apologetics. Second, he ranked Gilson among those Christian philosophers for whom only a "lived" knowledge of God was a true knowledge of Him. While this was a rank oversimplification of the position of Gilson, most attentive to the manifold distinctions between philosophy and faith, it was expressive of Jones' Methodist heritage centered on religious enthusiasm.

latter rested on two precepts. One implied the full recognition on the part of Christian philosophers that they were
practically alone (Gilson may have found ample proof of
this in the Gifford lectureship, by then half a century old, a
proof to be further strengthened by another half a century)
in holding the viability of a rational demonstration of the
existence of a personal Creator. They should, therefore,
unabashedly admit, Gilson kept arguing, the religious
provenance of this conviction of theirs, a provenance fully
attested from the earliest phases of Christian thought. The
other precept meant the no less emphatic recognition that in
spite of that provenance the demonstration in question and
the epistemology implied in it were fully accessible to
reason and that, in consequence, Christian philosophy was
genuinely philosophical. Tantalizing fragments of that
epistemology are available in some of Gilson's shorter
works, among them his *Réalisme méthodique* which is not
disconnected with the subsequent story of Gifford lectures.

Gilson, a Thomist's Thomist, was not the first to refer
to Thomism with distinct sympathy in the framework of
Gifford lectures. To do so was Taylor, also among the first
to speak in Great Britain of Gilson's *Etudes de philosophie
médiévale*. Taylor's broad espousal of Aristotelian realism
showed some Gilsonian parallel in that just as Gilson had to
overcome Bergsonism to discover realist metaphysics,
Taylor too had to find his way to it by extricating himself
from idealism which he had imbibed as a pupil of Green.
Taylor's espousal of High Church doctrines led him to
discuss in the second series of his lectures the connection
between natural theology and positive or Christian theology. In doing so he was advancing toward the position
which Gilson later articulated in his notion of "Christian
philosophy." Taylor, who devoted the first series of his
lectures to natural theology as suggested by problems of
ethics, was followed in his broadly Thomist approach by
De Burgh. The latter's principal claim, that modern ethical
relativism, which threatened the very fabric of civilization,
could only be cured by abandoning epistemologies intent
only on the practical and logical, had very much in view the
lectures of Ross, who denied that ethics had any transcendental ground.

Another series of lectures, even more emphatically antitheistic than the ones by Ross, was given by Dewey. In a repetitious and dull discourse Dewey presented any reasoning in search for antecedent metaphysical causes both as an illusory quest for certainty and also as the principal barrier to the relative security to be had through the scientific method. The latter consisted for Dewey in the ability to give man power to control his environment. Giving his lectures at the age of eighty, Dewey saw, not unexpectedly, the latest achievements in science, in particular Einstein's relativity, in the rigidly positivist perspective which he had worked out for himself half a century earlier. As if by irony it was while Dewey delivered his lectures that Einstein himself came to realize in full what others, such as Planck, had already noted publicly, namely, that relativity theory was anything but relativism and positivism. Rather, it was realist, nay absolutist, in its very foundations[45] and rested on that search for metaphysical antecedents which Dewey kept excoriating as a chief intellectual and cultural evil.

From the viewpoint of philosophy there is little of significance to be gathered in the lectures given by Niebuhr, Laird, and Kroner as World War II got under way. The "Christian" interpretation which Niebuhr tried to give to the nature and destiny of man was deprived of philosophical foundations and breadth by the short shrift given in his Barthian neo-orthodoxy to metaphysics and epistemology. Laird represented the speculative part of a rather antiquated Kantianism issuing in sceptical conclusions about natural theology in general and cosmology in particular. Of Einsteinian cosmology, which fully reinstated, *pace* Kant, the validity of the notion of the universe, Laird had no inkling. Kroner advocated Kant's insistence on the practical necessity of *believing*, with typically very little specific as to *what* one was to believe in.

45. For details, see chs. 11 and 12 of my Gifford lectures and my articles, "The Absolute beneath the Relative: Reflections on Einstein's Theories," *Intercollegiate Review* 25 (1985): 68–92, and "Planck's Epistemological Impasse," *Philosophia* (Athens), forthcoming.

The same predicament was the debilitating aspect of the lectures of Brunner, one of the first three to reactivate the Gifford lectures that ceased being given for six years owing to wartime conditions. For all his advocacy of a moderate form of neo-orthodoxy, which put him at acrimonious odds with Barth, Brunner had rough going in setting forth a philosophically articulate Christian notion of creation which alone, he claimed, could serve as a safe guideline out of cultural anarchy. Underlying that anarchy was, according to Brunner, the discrediting, in terms of Kantian agnosticism, of the notion of natural law. Clearly, Brunner wanted to take a position which went as much against Kroner's encomiums of Kant's program as against Barth's rejection of natural law, a rejection in which, Brunner pointedly noted, Barth unwittingly agreed with his chief antagonists, the Nazis. Brunner's own insistence on a genuine natural law was hampered by his diffidence about philosophy which he viewed as having, in the form of Neoplatonism, imprisoned the genuine Christian message from Patristic times on. Yet, he admitted that Gilson had made a serious case to the contrary view, namely, that Christian theology, both in its Augustinian and Thomistic forms, had made an effective and much needed use of Greek philosophy without compromising the sovereignty of the Creator.

Brunner's claim that Thomism was essentialist in the Platonist sense and therefore subservient to necessitarianism received an indirect rebuttal in the lectures of Gabriel Marcel, an early exponent of Christian existentialism in which the need for ontology was fully recognized. The chief aim of Marcel, who found in his Gifford lectureship an unexpected demand to give for the first time a systematic account of his thought, had always been to reawaken the sense of wonder about existence. Yet, when it came to the proofs of the existence of God, he did not elaborate on their real and only reliable ground: the same sense of wonder. This was all the more strange because Marcel specified the root of the apparent undemonstrativeness of those proofs in the modern mind's growing insensitivity about the wonder of existence, individual and cosmic. For that tragic process

Marcel laid special blame on the growing popularity of the Hegelian view of history.

The opposite of that insensitivity was the gist of the lectures of Dawson who, however, spoke not so much as a philosopher as a cultural historian. A major modern effort to overcome that insensitivity, though in strict disregard for Christian culture, was Perry's application of his theory of values to their entire realm. Since the insensitivity in question could be seen as the source of the rise of conflicting ideological, cultural, and social trends, it was not altogether unexpected that Perry held high "harmonious happiness" as the *summum bonum*. Not that Perry meant a superficial harmony. His apparently relativist notion of harmony rested on the absolutist and indeed metaphysical claim that all men shared in a common nature and therefore all were, in principle at least, capable of recognizing their best individual interest in an interest common to all men. But the realism of Perry was not rooted in the metaphysical wonder with respect to a nature existing universally beyond the individual. Consequently, the cosmic religious destiny he ascribed to man could not be given by him a convincingly theistic stamp. After all, Perry's chief idol was none other than James whose pluralism was a monism in disguise, a monism germane to Perry's realism.

Genuinely theistic stamp could not be the characteristic of the lectures of Blanshard who represented a militantly rationalist type of monism. A great deal of his energy was expended on a furious and at times patently unscholarly attack on positive Christianity and especially on Roman Catholicism. Thus while he quoted Lord Acton to the effect that "if a man accepts the Papacy with confidence . . . he must have made term with murder,"[46] he kept silent about Lord Acton's often made declaration that for him "communion with Rome was dearer than life."[47] To mention Canon Raven in the next breath has a far deeper reason than the fact that he gave his Gifford lectures about the same

46.   Blanshard, *Reason and Belief*, p. 96.
47.   See "The Challenge of Acton," by O. Chadwick, in *The Tablet*, Jan 28, 1984, p. 77.

time as Blanshard. While a first-rate naturalist and an enthusiast of Darwinism who had open eyes for facts with which it could not cope, Canon Raven was a dubious theologian to say the least. In his hands the relation between natural science and Christian theology headed toward a complete capitulation of all Christian dogmas, including the strict personality and transcendence of the Creator, to a scientifically coated cosmic evolutionism. Hardly more was to be expected from one who found in a well-drilled Cambridge eight a telling example of the Kingdom of God as preached by Jesus. Such theology was not even so good as to contain points with which a rationalist or agnostic could really disagree.

The same years provided the opposite case in the lectures of Tillich. He threw away the possibility of agreeing rationally about God or about anything relating to Him with his claim that God was so "other" as to be outside the category of being. Concerning the category of time, a similar extremist position was taken in the lectures of Bultmann who in his emphasis on Christian eschatology deprived of its significance the temporal.

Clearly, there was need for voicing a middle-road position concerning the credibility of Christian religion. The lectures of the Anglican Bishop Hodgson as well as those of the Scottish Presbyterian theologian Baillie had such an aim. Typically, both started with an analysis of faith as knowledge. Baillie ended his lectures with a strong note on his differing from Barth precisely on the point whether mankind ever had any knowledge of God outside the framework of biblical revelation. The epistemological status of belief in general was analyzed at considerable length in the lectures of Price who, however, stopped short of considering in detail the mental steps leading to the acknowledgment of God.

Several lectures were offered in the postwar years that would qualify as natural theologies in a systematic sense. MacMurray developed a theory of knowledge based on the notion of person with an emphasis on the ethical perception as a platform from which to recognize the existence of a personal God. Farrer centered on the reality and full specter of free will which he supported by a detailed presentation of the mind's immateriality. With less rigor was the argument from ethical consciousness pursued by Knox who made no secret of his being an essentially 19th-century thinker with no sympathy for post-Wittgensteinian philosophers. The latter and various spokesmen of contemporary situation ethics were very much in the mind of Mitchell who also differed from Knox in not being a Hegelian. Farmer, who started with an analysis of the relation between natural theology and philosophy and in particular of Christian philosophy as defined by Gilson, quickly turned his attention to a description and classification of religious types. The center of Campbell's arguments was his notion of symbolic knowledge whose relatedness to the Thomistic doctrine of analogy he did not fail to point out. In fact his lectures came to a close with an acknowledgement of Mascall's work on the analogy of being, written two decades before Mascall delivered his own Gifford lectures which deserve special attention.

Mascall did not try to conceal the fact that an essentially Thomistic natural theology faces two special problems, both derivative of a now several-century-old climate of thought. One is the overweening influence of rationalism and idealism in which the real has been equated with the logical. (For empiricism the real has largely become equivalent to what is describable in quantitative terms always translatable into terms of logic). The problem arising from this acts like a language barrier: basic words used by metaphysical realists prove ineffectual in conveying to opposite camps the intended meaning. A second problem is the necessity to persuade the idealist that in the very act whereby a thing becomes known it also reveals its non-necessary character. To overcome these difficulties Mascall probed the self-defeating aspects of linguistic and non-realist philosophies. A chief target of his was transcendental Thomism, an outgrowth of Maréchal's contention that Aquinas could be made relevant only by grafting on his thought Kant's critical method according to which, when taken rigorously, one can sit in judgment over knowledge before knowing something. Another strategy of Mascall was a recall of cases which show non-realist philosophers giving unwitting evidence to their awareness of the contingency of real things. Such a case is Wittgenstein's admission: "I had sometimes had a certain experience which could best be described by saying that 'when I have it *I wonder at the existence of the world'*."[48]

In making his basic philosophical points, Mascall drew heavily on Gilson's *Réalisme méthodique*, but at the same time he stayed content to prove only a knowledge of God which is "minimal in the extreme." For, as he remarked in the same breath, once "a point can be located in which finite being manifests the presence in it of the infinite, the knife-blade can be inserted and the cavity widened later on."[49] Books so far published by Swinburne suggest that his lectures when published will be such a widening. When that cavity is probed and re-articulated with non-realist conceptual tools, as done in Macquarrie's lectures, the results show the unintended uneasiness of being in the company of not entirely trustworthy thesis, such as Plotinus, Eriugena, Hegel and Whitehead. Macquarrie might have found better spokesmen for the apophatic-kataphatic dialectic of which he is particularly fond and which is, of course, very necessary in speaking about God.

Not so much a widening of the opening specified by Mascall as a display of its instructiveness in a different context was the aim of the lectures delivered by the author of this essay. He assumed as proven the cosmological argument, that is, a realist perception of the totality of consistently interacting things, or the universe, as thoroughly contingent, that is, one of the infinite number of possible universes owing its existence to a free creative act of God. Then he surveyed the history of the exact sciences and of the scientific methodologies to show that the great creative advances of science were made in terms of an epistemology akin to the epistemology implied in the

48. N. Malcolm, *Ludwig Wittgenstein: A Memoir*, with a biographical sketch by G. H. von Wright (London: Oxford University Press), 1958), p. 70.
49. Mascall, *The Openness of Being*, p. 14.

cosmological argument. The inverse of this conclusion is displayed when a philosophical position which vitiates the cosmological argument is used as a scientific methodology. The results are actually or potentially disastrous for science. But the most important contribution to natural theology which is provided by a historical analysis of science relates to the entry of cosmology into science in the 20th century. Whatever the Kantian objections to the validity of the notion of the universe, that validity is indispensable for modern scientific cosmology. Its theoretical constructs, which cannot become apriori and self-containing because of Gödel's theorems, bespeak the contingency of the universe no less than do the astonishingly specific features of the cosmos from its earliest phases on. A long way indeed from that infinite homogeneous universe which in Herbert Spencer's flowing prose appeared as a necessary being. On seeing the philosophical inertia of idealists and logicists to resist their arguments, advocates of natural theology should recall the baffling insensitivity to H. G. Wells' inimitable though forgotten unmasking, now half-a-century-old, of Spencer's self-contradictory effort: "He [Spencer] believed that individuality (heterogeneity) was and is an evolutionary product from an original homogeneity, begotten by folding and multiplying and dividing and twisting it, and still fundamentally *it*."[50] The *it*, of course, was that perfect homogeneity which is the very next thing to non-existence.

Opponents of theism found philosophical spokesmen among recent Gifford lecturers in Ayer and Findlay who were forced to their conclusions by the logical positivism they represented. In dealing with questions of ethics Wright was led, at least implicitly, to similar conclusions and for the same reason. The lectures of Arendt, the first woman to give Gifford lectures, ended in her voicing a frustrated bafflement over the irreducible fact of free will, which mitigated their Hegelian tone. Suggestive rather than demonstrative was the tone of Lewis and Copleston, historians of religion and of philosophy, respectively.

50. H. G. Wells, *First and Last Things: A Confession of Faith and Rule of Life* (London: Watts and Co., 1929), p. 30.

Copleston's lectures represented a first among Gifford lectures in having for their topic Eastern philosophy and mysticism. Clark, who offered a most convincing plea on behalf of realist metaphysics against the claims of positivism and linguistics, went on to rest the case of theism entirely on faith and on mystical experience.

For a philosophical theist it is always a help to find a prominent scientist oppose the materialist or reductionist exploitation of science. Such help was forthcoming from the first series of the lectures of Eccles and to a lesser degree from the lectures of Weizsäcker. Heisenberg concluded that science entitled one to nothing higher than reverent agnosticism. To see that agnosticism, if taken consistently, can hardly be anything, let alone a truly reverent attitude, is the kind of philosophical insight, though rather elementary, which is not necessarily perceived by a scientist, however eminent. He can in fact be shockingly insensitive to hoisting himself by his own petard. Thus Young, who devoted his lectures to a survey of recent brain research, a survey in stark contrast to Eccles' second series of lectures, dismissed religion as a mere matter of the wiring of religious people's brains. He failed to realize that non-religiosity could on that ground be no more than a lack of such wiring, or rather a matter of different wiring, and not at all a philosophically defensible position.

Among scientist Gifford lecturers, who made at least a brief reflection on natural theology, Polanyi, Hardy, and Thorpe represent positions worth considering to some extent. Behind Polanyi's reflections, not only brief but also studiedly vague, there lies the ambivalence of his advocacy of science as personal knowledge. Its effectiveness to undermine scientistic reductionism was attested by the unabashedly hostile reaction to it on the part of notoriously reductionist men of science. Yet, if all knowledge is essentially personal, the objectivity of knowledge can become doubtful not only in the scientific but also in any other domain, and to the extent of allowing but fleeting phrases about, say, natural theology. This implication was tacitly attested by the Gifford lectures of Polanyi who, tellingly enough, went on to celebrating the tacitness of the origin and foundation of all knowledge. The claim in Polanyi's Gifford lectures that the experience of a scientist making a discovery is akin to the experience of a Christian who worships God antedated by several years Polanyi's more than fleeting and, indeed, personal acquaintance with Christian worship. Hardy, the leader of "Religious Experience Research Unit" in Manchester College, Oxford, certainly proved that mystical proclivities are not in themselves enough to overcome the shallows of religious empiricism. The principal thrust of his lectures was a rehabilitation of Bergson's *élan vital* with the help of Teilhard de Chardin's spiritualization of Darwinism. The average reader of Hardy's lectures would more readily discard with him a specifically Christian theism than to see a truly transcendental God beyond the pan-evolutionary process apotheosized by him.

That a scientist need not necessarily be a professional student of natural theology in order to do far better than Hardy is well illustrated by the concluding chapter of Thorpe's vast survey of the differences between animal and human nature. For if the scientist's philosophical instincts are sound and his sensitivity for basic distinctions keen, he can find an articulate mouthpiece among philosophers and theologians still appreciative of natural theology. Thorpe certainly found one, Canon James Stanley Bezzant, Dean of St John's College, Cambridge, who spelled out the issue with rare forcefulness:

> Intellectual objections to Christianity nowadays, and the fact that there are at present no convincing answers to them, both grow out of one root. This is that there is no general or widely accepted natural theology. I know that many theologians rejoice that it is so and seem to think that it leaves them free to commend Christianity as Divine revelation. They know not what they do. For if the immeasurably vast and mysterious creation reveals nothing of its originator or of his or its attributes and nature, there is no *ground* whatever for supposing that any events recorded in an ancient and

partly mythopoeic literature, and deductions from it can do so.[51]

Natural theology was not visible in a number of lectures that recently had religion for their subject under such diverse aspects as the spiritual vitality of the patriarchate of Constantinople under Turkish domination (Runciman), the secularization of European mind in the 19th century (O. Chadwick), Bayle's grappling with the problem of evil (Jossua), Marxism as a directive for Christian renewal (van Leeuwen), mysticism in its global varieties (Zaehner), and the essentially sacred character of pre-modern thought in the East and the West (Nasr, the first Muslim Gifford lecturer). Smart's survey of world religions conjured up the demise of organized religion and the emergence of a global culture driven by a broadly religious mentality in which major religious traditions were so many complementary aspects. As one would expect, no specific conclusions emerged from two series of Gifford lectures organized as panel discussion among two philosophers of widely differing persuasions (Kenny and Lucas), a computer scientist (Longuet–Higgins), and a biologist (Waddington). Daiches was the first Gifford lecturer to concentrate on the thoughts which poets, belonging mostly in the Anglo-Saxon tradition, voiced about God and especially the God of the Bible. His lectures were permeated by the hope that such thoughts could be given justice in terms defined by David Hume who rejected the ontological validity of any proposition concerning God. Hume would have viewed with gentle irony Daiches' expectation that emotional experiences of God's reality would have any substance outside strictly subjective limits.

The lectures given during the last fifteen or twenty years displayed as great if not a greater variety of approaches than the ones given during the earlier decades. Some were

51. The quotation in Thorpe's *Animal Nature and Human Nature* (p. 382) is from Bezzant's contribution, "Intellectual Objections," to *Objections to Christian Belief*, edited by A. R. Vidler (London: Constable, 1963), p. 107.

monographs relating but vaguely to the stated aims of the Founder, others were a refutation of some claims which, if true, would render natural theology a patently hapless enterprise. Again, some others were but high-minded expressions of a humanistic agnosticism and at least one a direct denial of natural theology. Explicit defenses of natural theology were few and none of them as systematic and rigorous as it could have been. The question therefore may legitimately be raised whether the Founder's munificence has achieved its purpose. A positive reply to this question may be had from a look at the Gifford lectures as a British philosophical institution.

Of course, the lectures are such an institution only in a broad though not-at-all trivial sense. The latter has to do with the most philosophical of all British Institutions, the Aristotelian Society. It came into existence in the very same year that witnessed the beginning of the Gifford lectures. That among future Gifford lecturers there were nearly three score who were also members of that Society should not seem surprising in view of the eminently philosophical target of the lectureship. Nor should it be surprising, in view of the eminence quickly gained by the lectureship, that more than half the Presidents of the Aristotelian Society served also as Gifford lecturers. But a more telling consideration can be had from a survey of the many hundred papers published in its *Proceedings*[52] or presented at its symposia that began in 1918. While the Aristotelian Society had a much vaster interest than Aristotle's very wide philosophical concerns, Aristotelian topics have been fairly often the subject of those papers. Yet, hardly a handful of them, and certainly none of the Symposia, had for their subject the topic which Aristotle viewed as the supreme target and fundamental motivation of philosophical inquiry, the reasoned discourse about God.

This may appear, on a cursory view at least, a system-

---

52.   As can easily be seen by glancing through the over hundred-page-long subject index in *Synoptic Index to the Proceedings of the Aristotelian Society* (1900–1949), edited by J. W. Scott (Oxford: Basil Blackwell, 1954).

atic slighting by the Aristotelian Society of a most Aristotelian topic. Yet, it may reasonably be assumed that
within the Aristotelian Society in particular and among
British philosophers in general there had developed a tacit
consensus already around the turn of the century that the
philosophy known as natural theology received a quasi-
institutional forum in the Gifford lectureship. That forum
witnessed the presentation of a dozen or so lecture series
which upon publication quickly gained the reputation of
philosophical classics. Since several of them would not,
according to the admission of their authors, have been
written but for the stimulus of the lectureship, the latter's
contribution to philosophy should seem above doubt.

The more particular question whether the lectureship
has served the interest of natural theology is not separate
from the meaning of what constitutes a genuine and lasting
philosophical contribution of a so-called classic. That meaning is thoroughly misconstrued if a classic philosophical
work is taken for a work whose message is universally
agreed to. James' pluralism has never become more than an
opinion whatever the customary encomiums accorded to it.
Alexander's articulation of a space-time, which through a
subconscious *nisus* unfolds itself into a still unfolding God,
keeps eliciting admiring words but nothing vaguely resem-
bling a universal consent. The same holds true for
Whitehead's process philosophy and for Polanyi's personal
knowledge. In fact, the latter touched off a series of sharp
dissents aimed at preserving the objectivity of science.
Dewey's pragmatism, Royce's idealism, and Ayer's logical
positivism are so many illustrations of the transient popularity of philosophical systems, dominating as they may be in
their heyday. James' dismissal—epitome of countless similar
ones—of the proofs of the existence of God on the ground
that they have failed to elicit general consent,[53] is a boomer-
ang that returns with a deadly vengeance to philosophy
proper after taking its apparently mortal swipe at natural
theology and the realist metaphysics underlying it.

If truth is taken equal to consensus, one has to despair

53. James, *The Varieties of Religious Experience*, p. 437.

not only about theology but about philosophy too, and indeed about civilization itself, including freedom, democracy, and science as well. Recent developments in Western society had made abundantly clear that constitutional law can no longer assume a consensus about its philosophical foundations. While even a generation or two ago those foundations were almost unanimously believed in, today the case is very different. The increasingly pragmatic interpretation given by High Courts to basic constitutional points reflect the prevalent cultural consensus that there are only behavioral patterns, all equally void of intrinsic goodness. In view of this a dismissal of natural theology as a "sick man of Europe"[54] is a mere registering of surface symptoms which prevents one from making the in-depth diagnosis of an intellectually and ethically sick Europe and Western World, the traditional homes of natural theology. Thus the fact that discourses on natural theology prompted by the Gifford lectureships are a saddeningly far cry from even a modest measure of consensus should be seen as part of a much broader malaise.

To suggest a cure for that malaise is all the more legitimate in this context because more than one Gifford lecturer was prompted to do so. Whether that cure, the development of a broadly shared consensus in objective truth and values that transcend man, would come about is hardly a safe topic to elaborate on. However, the entire history of natural theology and certainly the history of Gifford lectures point to the intimate connection of natural theology with Christian theology as the source of that consensus. That Lord Gifford was unaware of that connection is not surprising. By the late 19th century the succession of Ockhamist occasionalism, Cartesian rational-

---

54. A phrase of N. Smart in his contribution "Revelation, Reason and Religions" to the Downside Conference (1959), published in Ian Ramsey (ed.), *Prospects for Metaphysics* (London: George Allen and Unwin, 1961). Smart proposed as a cure of the old and hard (because metaphysical) natural theology the replacement of it by a "soft one," which fully anticipated the syncretistic and pragmatist position set forth twenty years later in his Gifford lectures.

ism, Leibnizian optimism, Voltairian deism, Comtean positivism, and Hegelian idealism had made even the best scholars of the history of philosophy forgetful of that connection, let alone of its real nature. Yet, natural theology rose high above the uncertain heights assigned to it by Plato, Aristotle, and the Stoics only in virtue of a profoundly Christian awareness about a personal God—Creator, Lawgiver, and Judge—to which Christian theologians, from the 2nd-century apologists on, emphatically attributed full rationality. At the same time, in order to secure rationality to what was ultimate in intelligibility and being, they had to pay increasingly systematic attention to the very ground and entire structure of a rational knowledge of the real.

In charging both Luther and Calvin with disloyalty to the spirit of Reformation on account of their occasional recourse to natural theology, Barth merely served witness to the reluctance of most Christian theologians to cut their moorings from reason, for fear of undercutting their very credibility. Barth was certainly alone among Christian Gifford lecturers in inveighing against natural theology. He and his followers seem to be strangely myopic to a facet of the much heralded onset of a post-Christian age through the alleged complete secularization of the Western mind. The facet is the mobilization by the Gifford lectureship of eminent intellectuals who, without professing to be Christians, let alone practising Christians, keep bringing witness to the reluctance of the human spirit to settle with the mere temporal and material. Even anti-theistic Gifford lectures (in particular the ones by Dewey and Ayer in which the rejection of natural theology was given within a broadly articulated epistemological system) can easily touch off a hunger for something more solid and elevated on the part of judicious readers.

The Christian cultivator of natural theology can indeed rest assured that the human *anima* or mind is naturally Christian on account of its innermost and ineradicable aspirations for something higher. But he will have to be mindful of the observation that a professor of purely natural religion is a chimaera insofar as religion is thought of as having for its object the worship of a personal Creator.[55] In addition, he has to be attentive to several important connections. One is the very complex relation between constructing a proof and the art of convincing others about its demonstrativeness. Proofs are of a great variety. Some are easy to accept because they are trivial, such as the working out of mere identity relations to which belong most proofs in logic, geometry, and the exact sciences. Others are elusive in the measure in which they are subtle though not necessarily complicated. Such are the proofs of the real—from material reality through psychological, sociological, historical to metaphysical, ethical, and religious reality. In the same way, the art of convincing ranges from the facile to the almost impossibly difficult. Another connection is that between natural theology and Christian theology. While the propositions of natural theology are fully accessible to reason, they will appeal only to a reason tuned to that appreciation of the real which the dogma about the Word made Flesh nurtures in those accepting it. They will not be disturbed by still another connection which is between metaphysics as a reasoned discourse and religion as a lived experience of the entire man, including not only his reason but all his higher faculties. Precisely because of this they will appreciate that the connection between reason and faith has to be such as to do justice to both. Therefore they will not ask from either to render a service which is inappropriate. They will not ask reason or philosophy to accept on *faith* what can be *known*, or demand from philosophy to perform as an artist who aims at impressing rather than explaining. Philosophers, such as Heidegger and his enormous band of epigones, who force the language in order to enforce new perceptions, lose their

55. A variation on Dom John Chapman's memorable remark: "There is not and never has been in the world such a monster as a professor of purely natural religion. A human being falls lower or rises higher, but is never a simply *natural* man." From the first of a series of letters to a Jesuit scholastic in *The Spiritual Letters of Dom John Chapman*, edited by R. Hudleston, (London: Sheed and Ward 1954), p. 193.

clarity in the measure in which they yield to the urge of manhandling plain words.

Hardly any of these connections were surmised by Lord Gifford who with the naiveté of a zealous amateur in philosophy as well as theology hoped that natural theology would deliver far more than it actually can. That it can deliver much less than it really can is a widely shared view in the academic community, including its theological sector. That for the past hundred years that community has been receiving salutary reminders[56] to the contrary has much to do with Lord Gifford's inspired bequest. It represented the final and supreme witness to his lifelong conviction, amply demonstrated in words as well as deeds, that widely varied as human learning may be, its unitary foundation can only be had in a vision that perceives a pointer to the eternal and the divine in all that is truly human.

56.   Those reminders were effective only when given in a printed form. A study of the failure of two dozen or so Gifford lecturers to publish their lectures would have its own instructiveness. Here it should suffice to recall two cases. Shortly after having delivered his lectures, Professor Hendel had to reserve all his available time and energy to the care of his sick wife. Somewhat puzzling is in Raymond Aron's lengthy *Mémoires* (Paris: Julliard, 1983) the mere mention (p. 354) of his Gifford lectures. Aron not only spoke there in great detail about several of his lecture-series given in Europe and the United States, but also noted that in his early seventies, or a decade after his Gifford lectures, he still felt youthfully vigorous.

List of Gifford Lecturers
and the Gifford Lectures*

ADAM, James (1860–1907), Aberdeen 1904–06, Fellow and
   Senior Tutor, Emmanuel College, Cambridge, *The
   Religious Teachers of Greece*, edited with a memoir by his
   wife, Adela Marion Adam (Edinburgh: T. & T. Clark,
   1908), xix + lv + 467pp.

ALEXANDER, Samuel (1859–1938), Glasgow 1916–18, Professor of Philosophy, University of Manchester, *Space,
   Time, and Deity* (London: Macmillan and Co., 1920), 2
   vols, xvi + 347 and xiii + 437pp.

ARBIB, Michael A. (1940–   ), Edinburgh 1983–84, Professor of Computer Science, University of Mass-
   achusetts at Amherst, "The Construction of Reality"
   jointly with HESSE.

ARENDT, Hannah (1906–1975), Aberdeen 1972–74, Professor
   of Philosophy, New School for Social Research, New
   York City, *The Life of the Mind, One: Thinking, Two:
   Willing* (New York: Harcourt, Brace, Jovanovich,
   1978), 2 vols, xii + 258 and x + 277pp.

ARON, Raymond (1905–1984), Aberdeen 1965–66, Professor,
   Institut d'Etudes Politiques and Sorbonne, "On Histori-
   cal Consciousness in Thought and Action," I. "On
   Historical Consciousness in Thought: Understanding

* In this list, which ends with the academic year 1983–84, unpublished lectures are given in Roman type. For a list which gives, with
minor errors, separately the published and unpublished lectures until
1966–67, see B. E. Jones, *Earnest Enquirers after Truth: A Gifford Anthology*
(London: George Allen & Unwin 1970), pp. 209–17. Each lecturer's
academic position is given as the one which he had when delivering the
lectures.

the Past," 2. "On Historical Action: The Prince and the Planner".

AYER, Alfred J. (1910–   ), St Andrews 1972–73, Professor of Logic, Oxford, *The Central Questions of Philosophy* (New York: Holt Rinehart and Winston, 1973), x + 243pp.

BAILLIE, John (1886–1960), Edinburgh 1961–62, Professor of Divinity and Principal of New College, Edinburgh, *The Sense of the Presence of God* (London: Oxford University Press, 1962), ix + 269pp.

BALFOUR, Arthur James (1848–1930), Glasgow 1913–14 and 1922–23, Member of Parliament, *Theism and Humanism* (London: Hodder and Stoughton, 1915), xv + 274pp and *Theism and Thought: A Study of Familiar Beliefs* (London: Hodder and Stoughton, [1923]), xii + 281pp.

BARNES, Ernest William (1874–1953), Aberdeen 1927–29, Bishop of Birmingham, *Scientific Theory and Religion: The World Described by Science and Its Spiritual Interpretation* (Cambridge: University Press, 1933), xxi + 685pp.

BARNES, Winston Herbert Frederick (1909–   ), Edinburgh 1968–70, Vice-Chancellor, University of Liverpool, "Knowledge and Faith".

BARTH, Karl (1886–1969), Aberdeen 1937–38, Professor of Theology, University of Basel, *The Knowledge of God and the Service of God according to the Teaching of the Reformation: Recalling the Scottish Confession of 1560*, translated by J. L. M. Haire and Ian Henderson (London: Hodder and Stoughton, 1938), xxix + 255pp.

BERGSON, Henri (1859–1941), Edinburgh 1913–14, Professor, Collège de France, Paris, "The Problem of Personality".

BEVAN, Edwyn Robert (1870–1943), Edinburgh 1932–34, Lecturer in Hellenistic History and Literature, King's College, London, *Symbolism and Belief* (London: George Allen & Unwin, 1938), 391pp and *Holy Images: An Inquiry into Idolatry and Image-Worship in Ancient Pagan-*

ism and in Christianity (London: George Allen & Unwin, 1940), 184pp.

BIDEZ, Joseph (1867–1945), St Andrews 1938–39, Professor of Classical Philology and the History of Philosophy, University of Ghent, *Eos; ou, Platon et l'Orient* (Bruxelles: M. Hayez, 1945), 156 + 51pp.

BLANSHARD, Brand (1892–1966), St Andrews 1951–53, Stirling Professor of Philosophy, Yale University, *Reason and Goodness* (London: George Allen & Unwin, 1961), 451pp and *Reason and Belief* (London: George Allen & Unwin, 1974), 620pp.

BOHR, Niels Henrik David (1885–1962), Edinburgh 1949–50, Director, Institute of Theoretical Physics, Copenhagen, "Causality and Complementarity: Epistemological Lessons of Studies in Atomic Physics".

BOSANQUET, Bernard (1848–1923), Edinburgh 1910–12, Professor of Moral Philosophy, University of St Andrews, *The Principle of Individuality and Value* (London: Macmillan, 1912), xxxvii + 409pp and *The Value and Destiny of the Individual* (London: Macmillan, 1913), xxxii + 331pp.

BOUTROUX, Emil (1845–1921), Glasgow 1903–05, Professor of Philosophy, Sorbonne, *Science et religion dans la philosophie contemporaine* (Paris: Ernest Flammarion, 1908), 400pp, English translation by Jonathan Nield, *Science and Religion in Contemporary Philosophy* (London: Duckworth, 1909), xi + 400pp.

BRADLEY, Andrew Cecil (1851–1935), Glasgow 1907–08, Professor of Poetry, Oxford, *Ideals of Religion* (London: Macmillan, 1940), viii + 286pp.

BRENNER, Sydney (1927–   ), Glasgow 1979–80, Director, Laboratory of Molecular Biology, Cambridge, "The New Biology".

BRUCE, Alexander Balmain (1831–1899), Glasgow 1896–98, Professor of Apologetics and New Testament Exegesis, Free Church College, Glasgow, *The Providential Order of the World* (New York: Charles Scribner's Sons, 1899), viii + 346pp and *The Moral Order of the World in Ancient and Modern Thought* (New York: Charles Scribner's Sons, 1899), viii + 431pp.

BRUNNER, Emil (1899–1966), St Andrews 1946–48, Professor of Systematic and Practical Theology, University of Zurich, *Christianity and Civilization: First Part: Foundations* (London: Nisbet, 1948), xi + 167pp, *Christianity and Civilization: Second Part: Specific Problems* (London: Nisbet, 1949), ix + 143pp.

BULTMANN, Rudolf (1884–1976), Edinburgh 1954–55, Professor of Theology, University of Marburg, *History and Eschatology* (Edinburgh: University Press, 1957), ix + 171pp.

BUTTERFIELD, Herbert (1900–1979), Glasgow 1965–67, Regius Professor of Modern History, Cambridge, "Human Beliefs and the Development of Historical Writing," and "Historical Writing and Christian Beliefs".

CAIRD, Edward (1835–1908), St Andrews 1890–92, Professor of Moral Philosophy, University of Glasgow, *The Evolution of Religion* (Glasgow: James MacLehose and Sons, 1893), 2 vols, xv + 400pp and vii + 334pp, and Glasgow 1900–02, Master of Balliol College, Oxford, *The Evolution of Theology in the Greek Philosophers* (Glasgow: James MacLehose and Sons, 1904), 2 vols, xvii + 382pp and xi + 377pp.

CAIRD, John (1820–1898), Glasgow 1894–96, Principal, University of Glasgow, *The Fundamental Ideas of Christianity*, with a Memoir by Edward Caird (Glasgow: James MacLehose and Sons, 1899), 2 vols, cxli + 232pp and 297pp.

CAMPBELL, Charles Arthur (1897–1974), St Andrews 1953–55, Professor of Logic and Rhetoric, University of Glasgow, *On Selfhood and Godhood* (London: George Allen & Unwin, 1957), xxxvi + 436pp.

CAMPBELL, Lewis (1830–1908), St Andrews 1894–96, Emeritus Professor of Greek, University of St Andrews, *Religion in Greek Literature: A Sketch in Outline* (Longmans, Green and Co., 1898), x + 423pp.

CHADWICK, Henry (1920–   ), St Andrews 1962–64, Regius Professor of Divinity, Oxford, "Authority in the Early Church".

CHADWICK, Owen (1916–   ), Edinburgh 1973–74, Regius Professor of Modern History, Cambridge, *The Secularization of the European Mind in the Nineteenth Century* (Cambridge: University Press, 1975), 286pp.

CHARLTON, Donald Geoffrey (1925–   ), St Andrews 1982–83, Professor of French, University of Warwick, "New Images of the Natural, 1750–1800".

CLARK, Stephen, R. L. (1945–   ), Glasgow 1981–82, Lecturer of Philosophy, University of Liverpool, *From Athens to Jerusalem: The Love of Wisdom and the Love of God* (Oxford: Clarendon Press, 1984), vi + 232pp.

COPLESTON, Frederick Charles (1907–   ), Aberdeen 1979–81, Professor Emeritus of the History of Philosophy, University of London, *Religion and the One: Philosophies East and West* (London: Search Press, 1982), 281pp.

DAICHES, David (1912–   ), Edinburgh 1982–83, Director, Institute of Advanced Studies in the Humanities, Edinburgh University, *God and the Poets* (Oxford: Clarendon Press, 1984), 232pp.

DAUBE, David (1909–   ), Edinburgh 1962–64, Regius Professor of Civil Law, Oxford, "1. The Dead and the Doer in the Bible," "2. Law and Wisdom in the Bible".

DAWSON, Christopher (1889–1970), Edinburgh 1947–49, Writer, Historian, *Religion and Culture* (New York: Sheed and Ward, 1948), v + 225pp and *Religion and the Rise of Western Culture* (London: Sheed and Ward, 1950), xvi + 286pp.

DE BURGH, William George (1866–1943), St Andrews

1937–38, Professor Emeritus of Philosophy, University of Reading, *From Morality to Religion* (London: Macdonald and Evans, 1938), xxii + 352pp.

DEMANT, Vigo Auguste (1893–1983), St Andrews 1956–58, Regius Professor of Moral and Pastoral Theology, Oxford, "The Penumbra of Ethics. 1. The Religious Climate. 2. The Moral Career of Christendom".

DEWEY, John (1859–1952), Edinburgh 1928–29, Professor of Philosophy, Columbia University, *The Quest for Certainty: A Study of the Relation of Knowledge and Action* (New York: Minton, 1929), 318pp.

DIXON, William McNeile (1866–1946), Glasgow 1935–37, Professor of English Language and Literature, University of Glasgow, *The Human Situation* (London: Edward Arnold, 1937), 448pp.

DREW, Philip (1925–   ), Glasgow 1982–83, Professor of English Literature, University of Glasgow, "The Literature of Natural Man".

DRIESCH, Hans (1867–1941), Aberdeen 1906–08, Professor of Biology, University of Heidelberg, *The Science and Philosophy of Organism* (London: Adam and Charles Black, 1908), 2 vols, xiii + 329 and xvi + 381pp.

ECCLES, John C. (1903–   ), Edinburgh 1977–79, Distinguished Professor Emeritus of Neurobiology, State University of New York in Buffalo, *The Human Mystery* (Berlin: Springer International, 1979), xvi + 255pp and *The Human Psyche* (Berlin: Springer International, 1980), xv + 279pp.

EDDINGTON, Arthur Stanley (1882–1944), Edinburgh 1926–27, Plumian Professor of Astronomy, Cambridge, *The Nature of the Physical World* (Cambridge: University Press, 1928), xix + 361pp.

FAIRBAIRN, Andrew Martin (1838–1912), Aberdeen 1891–93, Principal, Mansfield College, Oxford, *The Philosophy of the Christian Religion* (New York: Macmillan Company, 1902), xxviii + 583pp.

FARMER, Herbert Henry (1892–   ), Glasgow 1949–50, Professor of Divinity, Cambridge, *Revelation and Religion: Studies in the Theological Interpretation of Religious Types* (London: Nisbet and Co., 1954), xi + 244pp.

FARNELL, Lewis Richard (1856–1934), St Andrews 1919–20 and 1924–25, Rector of Exeter College and Vice-Chancellor of the University of Oxford, *Greek Hero Cults and Ideas of Immortality* (Oxford: Clarendon Press, 1921), xv + 434pp and *The Attributes of God* (Oxford: Clarendon Press, 1925), x + 283pp.

FARRER, Austin Marsden (1904–1968), Edinburgh 1956–57, Fellow and Chaplain, Trinity College, Oxford, *The Freedom of the Will* (London: Adam and Charles Black, 1958), xi + 330pp.

FINDLAY, John Niemeyer (1903–   ), St Andrews 1964–66, Professor of Philosophy, King's College, University of London, *The Discipline of the Cave* (London: George Allen and Unwin, 1966), 227pp and *The Transcendence of the Cave* (London: George Allen and Unwin, 1967), 224pp.

FOWLER, William Warde (1847–1921), Edinburgh 1909–10, Tutor and Fellow of Lincoln College, Oxford, *The Religious Experience of the Roman People from the Earliest Times to the Age of Augustus* (London: Macmillan and Co., 1911), xviii + 504pp.

FRASER, Alexander Campbell (1819–1914), Edinburgh 1894–96, Professor of Logic and Metaphysics, University of Edinburgh, *Philosophy of Theism* (Edinburgh: William Blackwood and Sons, 1895–96), 2 vols, 303pp and xiii + 288pp.

FRAZER, James George (1854–1941), St Andrews 1911–13, Professor of Social Anthropology, University of Liverpool, *The Belief in Immortality and the Worship of the Dead. Vol. I. The Belief among the Aborigines of Australia, the Torres Straits Islands, New Guinea and Melanesia*

(London: Macmillan and Co., 1913), xxi + 495pp, and Edinburgh 1923–25, *The Worship of Nature. Volume I* (New York: The Macmillan Company, 1926), xxvi + 672pp.

GALLOWAY, Allan Douglas (1920–   ), Glasgow 1983–84, Professor Emeritus of Divinity, University of Glasgow, "God's Other Nature. The Humanity of God".

GILSON, Etienne (1884–1978), Aberdeen 1930–32, Professor, Collège de France, Paris, *L'esprit de la philosophie médiévale* (Paris: J. Vrin, 1932), 2 vols, viii + 329pp and 297pp, English translation by A. H. C. Downes, *The Spirit of Medieval Philosophy* (New York: Charles Scribner's Sons, 1936), ix + 490pp.

GORE, Charles (1853–1932), St Andrews 1929–30, Fellow of King's College, Sometime Bishop of Oxford, *The Philosophy of the Good Life* (London: John Murray, 1930), xiii + 342pp.

GWATKIN, Henry Melvill (1844–1916), Edinburgh 1903–05, Dixie Professor of Ecclesiastical History, Cambridge, *The Knowledge of God and Its Historical Development* (Edinburgh: T. & T. Clark, 1906) 2 vols, xi + 308 and 334pp.

HALDANE, John Scott (1860–1936), Glasgow 1926–28, Fellow of New College, Oxford, *The Sciences and Philosophy* (London: Hodder and Stoughton, 1929), ix + 344pp.

HALDANE, Richard Burdon (1856–1928), St Andrews 1902–04, Member of Parliament, *The Pathway to Reality* (London: John Murray, 1903–04), 2 vols, xix + 316pp and xxvii + 275pp.

HARDY, Alister Clavering (1896–1985), Aberdeen 1963–65, Professor Emeritus of Zoology, Oxford, *The Living Stream: A Restatement of Evolution Theory and Its Relation to the Spirit of Man* (London: Collins, 1965), 292pp and *The Divine Flame: An Essay towards a Natural History of Religion* (London: Collins, 1966), 254pp.

HEISENBERG, Werner Carl (1901–1976), St Andrews 1955–56, Director, Max Planck Institute, Göttingen, *Physics and Philosophy: The Revolution in Modern Science* (New York: Harper, 1958), 206pp.

HENDEL, Charles William (1890–1982), Glasgow 1962–63, Professor Emeritus, Yale University, "Politics, 1. The Trial of a Pelagian Faith, 2. The Limit of Human Power".

HENSON, Herbert Hensley (1863–1947), St Andrews 1935–36, Bishop of Durham, *Christian Morality: Natural, Developing, Final* (Oxford: Clarendon Press, 1936), xiv + 340pp.

HESSE, Mary Brenda (1924–   ), Edinburgh 1983–84, Professor of Philosophy of Science, Cambridge, *see* ARBIB.

HOBSON, Ernest William (1850–1933), Aberdeen 1920–22, Sadlerian Professor of Pure Mathematics, Cambridge, *The Domain of Natural Science* (Cambridge: University Press, 1923), xvi + 510pp.

HOCKING, William Ernest (1873–1966), Glasgow 1936–37, Professor of Philosophy, Harvard University, "Fact and Destiny".

HODGES, Herbert Arthur (1905–1976), Aberdeen 1955–57, Professor of Philosophy, University of Reading, "The Logic of Religious Thinking, 1. Its Customary Forms and Presuppositions, 2. Its Intellectual Status".

HODGSON, Leonard (1889–1969), Glasgow 1955–57, Regius Professor of Divinity, University of Oxford, *For Faith and Freedom* (Oxford: Basil Blackwell, 1956–57), 2 vols, vii + 241pp and 237pp.

HOOYKAAS, Reijer (1906–   ), St Andrews 1975–77, Professor of History of Science, University of Utrecht, "Fact, Faith and Fiction in the Development of Science".

HULTKRANTZ, Ake (1920–   ), Aberdeen 1981–83, Professor

of Comparative Religion, University of Stockholm, "The Veils of Religion: Religion in its Ecological Forms. 1. The Forms of Religion, 2. The Ecology of Religion".

INGE, William Ralph (1860–1954), St Andrews 1917–19, Dean of St. Paul's, London, Formerly Lady Margaret Professor of Divinity, Cambridge, *The Philosophy of Plotinus* (London: Longmans, Green and Co., 1918), 2 vols, xvi + 270 and xii + 253pp.

JAEGER, Werner (1899–1961), St Andrews 1936–37, Professor of Greek and Ancient Philosophy, University of Chicago, *The Theology of the Early Greek Philosophers* (Oxford: Clarendon Press, 1947), vii + 259pp.

JAKI, Stanley L. (1924–   ), Edinburgh 1974–76, Distinguished University Professor, Seton Hall University, South Orange NJ, *The Road of Science and the Ways to God* (Chicago: University of Chicago Press, 1978), vii + 478pp.

JAMES, William (1842–1910), Edinburgh 1900–02, Professor of Philosophy, Harvard University, *The Varieties of Religious Experience: A Study of Human Nature* (London: Longmans, Green and Co., 1902), xii + 534pp.

JONES, Henry (1853–1922), Edinburgh 1919–21, Professor of Moral Philosophy, University of Glasgow, *A Faith that Enquires* (New York: The Macmillan Co., 1922), x + 278pp.

JOSSUA, Jean Pierre (1930–   ), Edinburgh 1976–77, Professor of Dogmatics, Faculté de théologie, Saulchoir, *Pierre Bayle ou l'obsession du mal* (Paris: Aubier Montaigne, 1977), 187pp.

KENNY, Anthony J. P. (1931–   ), Edinburgh 1971–73, Fellow, Balliol College, Oxford, *The Nature of Mind* (Edinburgh: University Press, 1972), 155pp and *The Development of Mind* (Edinburgh: University Press, 1973), 151pp, *jointly with* LONGUET-HIGGINS, LUCAS, and WADDINGTON.

KOHLER, Wolfgang (1887–1967), Edinburgh 1957–59, Professor of Psychology, Swarthmore College, PA, "1. The Psychology of Values, 2. Psychology and Physics".

KNOX, Thomas Malcolm (1900–1980), Aberdeen 1966–68, Principal of the University of St. Andrews, *Action* (London: George Allen & Unwin, 1968), 250pp and *A Layman's Quest* (London: George Allen & Unwin, 1969), 187pp.

KRAUS, Oscar (1872–1942), Edinburgh 1940–41, Formerly Professor of Philosophy, University of Prague, "New Meditations on Mind, God, and Creation".

KRONER, Richard (1884–1974), St Andrews 1939–40, Formerly Professor of Philosophy, University of Kiel, *The Primacy of Faith* (New York: Macmillan Company, 1943), xi + 226pp.

LAIRD, John (1887–1946), Glasgow 1938–40, Regius Professor of Moral Philosophy, University of Aberdeen, *Theism and Cosmology* (London: George Allen and Unwin, 1940), 325pp and *Mind and Deity* (London: George Allen and Unwin, 1941), 322pp.

LANCIANI, Rodolfo Amadeo (1846–1929), St Andrews 1899–1901, Professor of Ancient Topography, University of Rome, *New Tales of Old Rome* (Boston: Houghton, Mifflin and Company, 1901), xii + 336pp.

LANG, Andrew (1844–1912), St Andrews 1888–90, Sometime Fellow of Merton College, Oxford, *The Making of Religion* (New York: Longmans, Green and Company, 1898), 380pp.

LARNER, Christina J. (1933–1983), Glasgow 1981–82, Reader in Psychology, University of Glasgow, *The Thinking Peasant: Popular and Educated Belief in Pre-Industrial Culture* (Glasgow: Pressgang, 1982), 93pp.

LAURIE, Simon Somerville (1829–1909), Edinburgh 1905–06, Professor of Education, University of Edinburgh, *On God and Man* (London: Longmans, Green and

Company, 1906), x + 416pp (Vol. II, Book II of his *Synthetica*).

LEEUWEN, van, Arend Theodoor (1918–   ), Aberdeen 1970–72, Associate Professor of Christian Ethics, Catholic University of Nijmegen, *Critique of Heaven* (London: Lutterworth Press, 1972), 206pp and *Critique of Earth* (Guildford: Lutterworth Press, 1974), 295pp.

LEWIS, Hywel David (1910–   ), Edinburgh 1966–68, Professor of History and Philosophy of Religion, University of London, *The Elusive Mind* (London: George Allen and Unwin, 1969), 347pp, *The Elusive Self* (London: The Macmillan Press, 1982), viii + 202pp, and *Freedom and Alienation* (Edinburgh: Scottish Academic Press, 1985), x + 162pp.

LONGUET-HIGGINS, Hugh Christopher (1923–   ), Edinburgh 1971–73, Professor of Theoretical Physics, University of Edinburgh, *see* KENNY.

LUCAS, John Randolph (1929–   ), Edinburgh 1971–73, Fellow, Merton College, Oxford, *see* KENNY.

MACKINNON, Donald Mackenzie (1913–   ), Edinburgh 1964–66, Norris-Hulse Professor of Divinity, Cambridge, "The Problem of Metaphysics".

MACBEATH, Alexander Murray (1888–1964), St Andrews 1948–49, Professor of Logic and Metaphysics, Queen's University, Belfast, *Experiments in Living: A Study of the Nature and Foundation of Ethics and Morals in the Light of Recent Work in Social Anthropology* (London: Macmillan and Company, 1952), xi + 462pp.

MACLENNAN, Roderick Diarmid (1898–1977), Edinburgh 1959–60, Minister, Church of Scotland, "The Unity of Moral Experience".

MACMURRAY, John (1891–1976), Glasgow 1952–54, Professor of Moral Philosophy, University of Edinburgh, *The Self as Agent* (London: Faber and Faber, 1957), 230pp and *Persons in Relation* (London: Faber and Faber, 1961), 235pp.

MACQUARRIE, John (1919–   ), St Andrews 1983–84, Lady Margaret Professor of Divinity, Oxford, *In Search of Deity: An Essay in Dialectical Theism* (London: SCM Press, 1984), x + 274pp.

MARCEL, Gabriel (1889–1973), Aberdeen 1948–50, Writer and Philosopher, *The Mystery of Being—I. Reflection & Mystery*, translated by G. S. Fraser (London: The Harvill Press, 1950), xiv + 219pp and *II. Faith & Reality*, translated by R. Hague (London: The Harvill Press, 1951), viii + 188pp.

MARETT, Robert Ranulph (1866–1943), St Andrews 1930–32, Rector of Exeter College, Oxford, *Faith, Hope and Charity in Primitive Religion* (New York: Macmillan Company, 1932), 239pp and *Sacraments of Simple Folk* (Oxford: Clarendon Press, 1933), 230pp.

MASCALL, Eric Lionel (1905–   ), Edinburgh 1970–71, Professor of Historical Theology, University of London, *The Openness of Being: Natural Theology Today* (Philadelphia: Westminster Press, 1971), xiii + 278pp.

MITCHELL, Basil George (1917–   ), Glasgow 1974–76, Nolloth Professor of the Philosophy of Christian Religion, Oxford, *Morality, Religious and Secular: The Dilemma of the Traditional Conscience* (Oxford: University Press, 1980), ix + 168pp.

MITCHELL, William (1861–1962), Aberdeen 1924–26, Professor of Philosophy, University of Adelaide, *The Place of Minds in the World. First Series* (London: Macmillan and Company, 1933), xxv + 374pp (Second Series, "The Power of Minds in the World").

MORGAN, Conwy Lloyd (1852–1936), St Andrews 1921–22, Professor Emeritus of Zoology and Geology, University of Bristol, *Emergent Evolution* (London: Williams and Norgate, 1923), xii + 313pp.

MÜLLER, Friedrich Max (1823–1900), Glasgow 1888–92, Professor of Comparative Philology, Oxford, *Natural Religion* (London: Longmans, Green and Co., 1889), xix + 608pp, *Physical Religion* (London: Longmans, Green and Co., 1891), xii + 410pp, *Anthropological Religion* (London: Longmans, Green and Co., 1892), xxvii + 464pp, *Theosophy or Psychological Religion* (London: Longmans, Green and Co., 1903), xxiii + 585pp.

MURDOCH, Iris (1919–   ), Edinburgh 1981–82, Fellow St. Ann's College, Oxford, "Metaphysics as a Guide to Morals".

NASR, Seyyed Hossein (1933–   ), Professor of Religion, Temple University, Philadelphia, *Knowledge and the Sacred* (Edinburgh: University Press, 1981), ix + 341pp.

NIEBUHR, Reinhold (1892–1971), Edinburgh 1938–40, Professor of Ethics and Theology, Union Theological Seminary, New York, *The Nature and Destiny of Man*: *A Christian Interpretation—I. Human Nature* (New York: Charles Scribner's Sons, 1941), xii + 306pp, *II. Human Destiny* (New York: Charles Scribner's Sons 1943), xii + 329pp.

NOCK, Arthur Darby (1902–1963), Aberdeen 1939–40 and 1946–47, Frothingham Professor of History of Religion, Harvard University, "Hellenistic Religion—The Two Phases".

PATERSON, William Paterson (1860–1939), Glasgow 1923–25, Professor of Divinity, University of Edinburgh, *The Nature of Religion* (London: Hodder and Stoughton, 1925), xii + 508pp.

PATON, Herbert James (1887–1969), St Andrews 1949–50, White's Professor Emeritus of Moral Philosophy, Oxford, *The Modern Predicament*: *A Study in the Philosophy of Religion* (London: George Allen & Unwin, 1955), 405pp.

PERRY, Ralph Barton (1876–1957), Glasgow 1946–48, Edgar Pierce Professor Emeritus of Philosophy, Harvard University, *Realms of Value*: *A Critique of Human Civilization* (Cambridge, Mass: Harvard University Press, 1954), xii + 497pp.

PFLEIDERER, Otto (1839–1908), Edinburgh 1892–94, Professor of Theology, University of Berlin, *Philosophy and Development of Religion* (Edinburgh: W. Blackwood & Sons, 1894), 2 vols, 331 and 459pp.

POLANYI, Michael (1891–1976), Aberdeen 1951–52, Professor of Social Studies, University of Manchester, *Personal Knowledge: Towards a Post-critical Philosophy* (Chicago: University of Chicago Press, 1958), xiv + 428pp.

PRICE, Henry Habberley (1899–1984), Aberdeen 1959–61, Wykeham Professor of Logic, Oxford, *Belief* (London: George Allen & Unwin, 1969), 495pp.

PRINGLE-PATTISON, Andrew [SETH] (1856–1931), Aberdeen 1911–13, Professor of Logic and Metaphysics, University of Edinburgh, *The Idea of God in the Light of Recent Philosophy* (Oxford: Clarendon Press, 1917), xvi + 423pp, and Edinburgh 1921–23, *The Idea of Immortality* (Oxford: Clarendon Press, 1922), xii + 210pp.

RAMSAY, William Mitchell (1851–1939), Edinburgh 1915–16, Sometime Regius Professor of Humanity, Aberdeen, *Asianic Elements in Greek Civilization* (London: John Murray, 1927), x + 303pp.

RAVEN, Charles Earle (1885–1964), Edinburgh 1950–52, Regius Professor Emeritus of Divinity, Cambridge, *Natural Religion and Christian Theology* (Cambridge: University Press, 1953), 2 vols, 224 and 227pp.

RIDGEWAY, William (1853–1926), Aberdeen 1909–11, Brereton Reader in Classics, Cambridge, "The Evolution of Religions of Ancient Greece and Rome".

ROSS, William David (1877–1971), Aberdeen 1935–36, Provost of Oriel College, Oxford, *Foundations of Ethics* (Oxford: Clarendon Press, 1939), xvi + 328pp.

ROYCE, Josiah (1855–1916), Aberdeen 1898–1900, Professor of History of Philosophy, Harvard University, *The World and the Individual. First Series: The Four Historical Conceptions of Being* (New York: Macmillan Company, 1900), xvi + 588pp and *Second Series: Nature, Man and the*

Moral Order (New York: Macmillan Company, 1901), xx + 480pp.

RUNCIMAN, Steven (1903–   ), St Andrews 1960–62, Fellow of Trinity College, Cambridge, *The Great Church in Captivity: A Study of the Patriarchate of Constantinople from the Eve of the Turkish Conquest to the Greek War of Independence* (Cambridge: University Press, 1968), x + 455pp.

SANFORD, Anthony J. (1944–   ), Glasgow 1982–83, Professor of Psychology, University of Glasgow, *Models, Mind and Man* (Glasgow: Pressgang, 1983), 101pp.

SAYCE, Archibald Henry (1845–1933), Aberdeen 1900–02, Professor of Assyriology, Oxford, *The Religions of Ancient Egypt and Babylonia* (Edinburgh: T. & T. Clark, 1903), vii + 509pp.

SCHWEITZER, Albert (1875–1965), Edinburgh 1934–35, Missionary Doctor, "The Problem of Natural Theology and Natural Ethics".

SHERRINGTON, Charles Scott (1857–1952), Edinburgh 1937–38, Sometime Professor of Physiology, Oxford, *Man on His Nature* (Cambridge: University Press, 1940), 413pp.

SMART, Ninian Roderick (1927–   ), Edinburgh 1979–80, Professor of Religious Studies, University of California, *Beyond Ideology: Religion and the Future of Western Civilization* (New York: Harper and Row, 1981), 350pp.

SMITH, John Alexander (1863–1939), Glasgow 1929–31, Waynflete Professor of Mental Philosophy, Oxford, "The Heritage of Idealism".

SÖDERBLOM, Nathan (1866–1931), Edinburgh 1930–31, Archbishop of Upsala, *The Living God: Basal Forms of Personal Religion*, with a biographical introduction by Dr. Y. Brilioth (London: Oxford University Press, 1933), xxix + 398pp.

SORLEY, William Ritchie (1855–1935), Aberdeen 1913–15,

Knightbridge Professor of Moral Philosophy, Cambridge, *Moral Values and the Idea of God* (Cambridge: University Press, 1919), xix + 534pp.

SOUTHERN, Richard William (1912–   ), Glasgow 1970–72, President, St. John's College, Oxford, "The Rise and Fall of the Medieval System of Religious Thought".

STAFFORD-CLARK, David (1916–   ), St Andrews 1977–78, Consultant, Department of Psychiatry, Guy's Hospital, London, "Myth, Magic and Denial: The Treacherous Allies".

STIRLING, James Hutchison (1820–1909), Edinburgh 1888–90, Writer and Philosopher, *Philosophy and Theology* (Edinburgh: T. & T. Clark, 1890), xvi + 407pp.

STOKES, George Gabriel (1819–1903), Edinburgh 1891–93, Lucasian Professor of Mathematics, Cambridge, *Natural Theology* (London: Adam and Charles Black, 1891–93), 2 vols, viii + 272 and viii + 272pp.

STOUT, George Frederick (1860–1944), Edinburgh 1919–21, Professor of Logic and Metaphysics, University of St Andrews, *Mind and Matter* (Cambridge: University Press, 1931), xiv + 325pp and *God and Nature*, edited by A. K. Stout with a memoir by J. A. Passmore (Cambridge: University Press, 1952), liv + 339pp.

SWINBURNE, Richard G. (1934–   ), Aberdeen 1982–84, Professor of Philosophy, University of Keele, "Man, 1. Body and Soul, 2. The Evolution of Man".

TAYLOR, Alfred Edward (1869–1945), St Andrews 1926–28, Professor of Moral Philosophy, University of Edinburgh, *The Faith of a Moralist. Series I. The Theological Implications of Morality. Series II. Natural Theology and the Positive Religions* (London: Macmillan and Company, 1932), xx + 437 and xxii + 437pp.

TEMPLE, William (1881–1944), Glasgow 1932–34, Archbishop of York, *Nature, Man and God* (London: Macmillan and Company, 1934), xxxii + 530pp.

THOMSON, John Arthur (1861–1933), St Andrews 1914–16, Regius Professor of Natural History, University of Aberdeen, *The System of Animate Nature* (London: Williams and Norgate, 1920), xi + 347pp.

THORPE, William Homan (1902–   ), St Andrews 1969–71, Professor Emeritus of Animal Ethology, *Animal Nature and Human Nature* (London: Methuen and Company, 1974), xix + 435pp.

TIELE, Cornelius Petrus (1830–1902), Edinburgh 1896–98, Professor of the History and Philosophy of Religion, University of Leiden, *Elements of the Science of Religion. Part I. Morphological* (New York: Charles Scribner's Sons, 1897), viii + 302pp and *Part II. Ontological* (New York: Charles Scribner's Sons, 1899), vi + 286pp.

TILLICH, Paul (1866–1965), Aberdeen 1952–54, Professor of Philosophical Theology, Union Theological Seminary, New York, *Systematic Theology. Volume II. Existence and the Christ* (Chicago: University of Chicago Press, 1957), xi + 187pp and *Volume III. Life and the Spirit. History and the Kingdom of God* (Chicago: University of Chicago Press, 1963), ix + 434pp.

TOYNBEE, Arnold Joseph (1889–1975), Edinburgh, 1952–53, Research Professor of International History, University of London, *An Historian's Approach to Religion* (London: Oxford University Press, 1956), ix + 317pp.

TYLOR, Edward Burnett (1832–1917), Aberdeen 1889–91, Keeper of the University Museum and Reader in Anthropology, Oxford.

VLASTOS, Gregory (1907–   ), St Andrews 1980–81, Stuart Professor Emeritus of Philosophy, Princeton University, "The Philosophy of Socrates".

WADDINGTON, Conrad Hal (1905–1975), Edinburgh 1971–73, Professor of Genetics, University of Edinburgh, *see* KENNY.

WALLACE, William (1844–97), Glasgow 1892–94, Whyte's Professor of Moral Philosophy, Oxford, *Lectures and*

Essays on Natural Theology and Ethics, edited with a biographical introduction by E. Caird (Oxford: Clarendon Press, 1898), xl + 566pp.

WARD, James (1843–1925), Aberdeen 1896–98, Professor of Mental Philosophy and Logic, Cambridge, *Naturalism and Agnosticism* (London: Macmillan and Company, 1899), 2 vols, xviii + 302 and xiii + 294pp, and St Andrews 1907–09, *The Realm of Ends or Pluralism and Theism* (New York: G. P. Putnam's Sons, 1911), xv + 490pp.

WATSON, John (1847–1939), Glasgow 1910–12, Professor of Moral Philosophy, Queen's University, Kingston, Canada, *The Interpretation of Religious Experience. Part First. Historical* (Glasgow: James Maclehose and Sons, 1912), xiv + 375pp and *Part Second. Constructive* (Glasgow: James Maclehose and Sons, 1912), x + 342pp.

WEBB, Clement Charles Julian (1865–1954), Aberdeen 1917–19, Fellow of Magdalen College, Oxford, *God and Personality* (London: George Allen and Unwin, 1918), 281pp and *Divine Personality and Human Life* (London: George Allen & Unwin, 1920), 291pp.

WEIZSÄCKER, Carl Friedrich von (1912–   ), Glasgow 1959–61, Professor of Philosophy, University of Hamburg, *The Relevance of Science: Creation and Cosmogony* (New York: Harper and Row, 1964), 192pp.

WHITEHEAD, Alfred North (1861–1947), Edinburgh 1927–28, Professor of Philosophy, Harvard University, *Process and Reality: An Essay in Cosmology* (Cambridge: University Press, 1929), xxiii + 509pp.

WISDOM, John (1904–   ), Aberdeen 1948–50, Lecturer in Moral Science, Cambridge, "1. The Mystery of the Transcendental, 2. The Discovery of the Transcendental".

WRIGHT, Georg Henrik von (1916–   ), St Andrews 1958–60, Professor of Philosophy, University of Helsinki, *Norm and Action: A Logical Inquiry* (London:

Routledge and Kegan Paul, 1963), xviii + 214pp, and *The Varieties of Goodness* (London: Routledge and Kegan Paul, 1963), xiv + 222pp.

ZAEHNER, Robert Charles (1913–1974), St Andrews 1967–69, Professor of Eastern Religions and Ethics, Oxford, *Concordant Discord: The Interdependence of Faiths* (Oxford: Clarendon Press, 1970), 464pp.

YOUNG, John Zachary (1907–   ), Aberdeen 1975–77, Professor Emeritus of Anatomy and Embryology, University College, London, *Programs of the Brain* (Oxford: University Press, 1978), 325pp.

★   ★   ★

Gifford lecturers who could not deliver their lectures because of sickness or death:

FLINT, Robert (1838–1910), Edinburgh 1907–09, Professor of Divinity, University of Edinburgh.

HUGEL, Friedrich von (1852–1925), Edinburgh 1924–26, Writer, Philosopher and Theologian.

The list of those who accepted the invitation to serve as Gifford lecturers but subsequently tendered their resignation for reasons other than health would include R. Otto and J. Maritain.

SYNOPTIC CHRONOLOGICAL LIST OF GIFFORD LECTURERS AT THE FOUR SCOTTISH UNIVERSITIES

	EDINBURGH	GLASGOW	ST ANDREWS	ABERDEEN
1888–89	Stirling	Müller	Lang	
1889–90	Stirling	Müller	Lang	Tylor
1890–91	Stokes	Müller	Caird E.	Tylor
1891–92	Stokes	Müller	Caird E.	Fairbairn
1892–93	Pfleiderer	Wallace		Fairbairn
1893–94	Pfleiderer	Wallace		
1894–95	Fraser	Caird J.	Campbell L.	
1895–96	Fraser	Caird J.	Campbell L.	
1896–97	Tiele			Ward
1897–98	Tiele	Bruce		Ward
1898–99				Royce
1899–1900			Lanciani	Royce
1900–01	James	Caird E.	Lanciani	Sayce
1901–02	James	Caird E.		Sayce
1902–03			Haldane R. B.	
1903–04	Gwatkin	Boutroux	Haldane R. B.	
1904–05	Gwatkin	Boutroux		Adam
1905–06	Laurie			Adam
1906–07				
1907–08		Bradley	Ward	Driesch
1908–09			Ward	Driesch
1909–10	Fowler			Ridgeway
1910–11	Bosanquet	Watson		Ridgeway
1911–12	Bosanquet	Watson	Frazer	Pringle-Pattison
1912–13			Frazer	Pringle-Pattison
1913–14	Bergson	Balfour		Sorley
1914–15		Balfour	Thomson	Sorley
1915–16	Ramsay		Thomson	
1916–17		Alexander		

	EDINBURGH	GLASGOW	ST ANDREWS	ABERDEEN
1917–18		Alexander	Inge	Webb
1918–19			Inge	Webb
1919–20	Stout	Jones	Farnell	
1920–21	Stout	Jones		
1921–22	Pringle-Pattison		Morgan	Hobson
1922–23	Pringle-Pattison	Balfour		
1923–24		Paterson		
1924–25		Paterson	Farnell	Mitchell
1925–26				Mitchell
1926–27	Eddington		Taylor	
1927–28	Whitehead	Haldane J. S.	Taylor	Barnes
1928–29	Dewey			Barnes
1929–30		Smith	Gore	
1930–31	Söderblom	Smith		Gilson
1931–32				Gilson
1932–33	Bevan	Temple	Marett	
1933–34	Bevan	Temple		
1934–35	Schweitzer			
1935–36		Dixon	Henson	Ross
1936–37		Dixon	Jaeger	Barth
1937–38	Sherrington	Hocking	De Burgh	Barth
1938–39	Niebuhr	Laird	Bidez	Nock
1939–40	Niebuhr	Laird	Kroner	
1940–41	Kraus			
1941–42				
1942–43				
1943–44				
1944–45				
1945–46				
1946–47		Perry	Brunner	Nock
1947–48	Dawson	Perry	Brunner	Wisdom
1948–49	Dawson		Macbeath	Marcel
1949–50	Bohr		Macbeath	Marcel
1950–51	Raven			
1951–52	Raven		Blanshard	Polanyi
1952–53	Toynbee	Macmurray	Blanshard	Tillich
1953–54		Macmurray	Campbell C. A.	Tillich
1954–55	Bultmann		Campbell C. A.	
1955–56		Hodgson	Heisenberg	
1956–57	Farrer	Hodgson	Demant	Hodges

	EDINBURGH	GLASGOW	ST ANDREWS	ABERDEEN
1957–58	Kohler		Demant	Hodges
1958–59	Kohler		Wright	
1959–60	McLennan	Weizsäcker	Wright	
1960–61			Runciman	Price
1961–62	Baillie		Runciman	Price
1962–63	Daube	Hendel	Chadwick	
1963–64	Daube		Chadwick	
				Hardy
1964–65	Mackinson		Findlay	Hardy/Aron
1965–66	Mackinson	Butterfield	Findlay	Aron
1966–67	Lewis	Butterfield		Knox
1967–68	Lewis		Zaehner	Knox
1968–69	Barnes W.		Zaehner	
1969–70	Barnes W.			Leeuwen
1970–71	Mascall		Thorpe	
1971–72	Kenny★	Southern		
1972–73	Kenny★		Ayer	Arendt
1973–74	Chadwick O.			Arendt
1974–75	Jaki	Mitchell		
1975–76	Jaki		Hooykaas	Young
1976–77	Jossua		Hooykaas	Young
1977–78	Eccles		Stafford-Clark	
1978–79	Eccles			
1979–80	Smart	Brenner		Copleston
1980–81	Nasr		Vlastos	Copleston
1981–82	Murdoch	Clark/Larner		Hultkrantz
1982–83	Daiches	Sanford/Drew	Charlton	Hultkrantz/ Swinburne
1983–84	Arbib/Hesse	Galloway	Macquarrie	Swinburne

★ Jointly with Longuet–Higgins, Lucas, and Waddington.

Lord Gifford's Will

TRUST DISPOSITION and SETTLEMENT of the late Adam Gifford, sometime one of the Senators of the College of Justice, Scotland, dated 21st August 1885.

I ADAM GIFFORD, sometime one of the Senators of the College of Justice, Scotland, now residing at Granton House, near Edinburgh, being desirous to revise, consolidate, alter, and amend my trust-settlements and testamentary writings, and having fully and maturely considered my means and estate, and the circumstances in which I am placed, and the just claims and expectations of my son and relatives, and the modes in which my surplus funds may be most usefully and beneficially expended, and considering myself bound to apply part of my means in advancing the public welfare and the cause of truth, do hereby make my Trust-deed and latter Will and Testament—that is to say, I give my body to the earth as it was before, in order that the enduring blocks and materials thereof may be employed in new combinations; and I give my soul to God, in Whom and with Whom it always was, to be in Him and with Him for ever in closer and more conscious union; and with regard to my earthly means and estate, I do hereby give, grant, dispone, convey, and make over and leave and bequeath All and Whole my whole means and estate, heritable and moveable, real and personal, of every description, now belonging to, or that shall belong to me at the time of my death, with all writs and vouchers thereof, to and in favour of Herbert James Gifford, my son; John Gifford, Esquire, my brother; Walter Alexander Raleigh, my nephew, presently residing in London; Adam West Gifford, W. S., my nephew; Andrew Scott, C. A., in Edinburgh, husband of my niece; and Thomas Raleigh, Esquire, barrister-at-law, London, and the survivors and survivor of them accepting, and the heirs of the last survivor, and to such other person or persons as I may name, or as may be assumed or appointed by competent authority, a majority being always a quorum, as trustees for the ends, uses, and purposes aftermentioned, but in trust only for the purposes following: That is to say, *First*, For payment of all my just and lawful debts, deathbed and funeral expenses, and the expense of executing this trust. *Second*, For payment to each trustee who may survive me, and accept and act as trustee, of the sum of £100 sterling, as a mere compliment and acknowledgment for his kindness in acting as trustee, but not as remuneration. *Third*, My trustees will see that my son, the said Herbert James Gifford, receives from the trustees appointed by the ante-nuptial contract of marriage between me and my late dear wife, the sum of £7400, or such other sum as may be in the hands of the said marriage contract trustees, as the whole amount of my dear wife's separate fortune, in terms of the said marriage contract in all respects. This sum of £7400 does not form part of my estate, but it is right to keep it in view in relation to the provisions in favour of the said Herbert James Gifford, my son. *Fourth*, To make payment to the said Herbert James Gifford of the sum of £5000 sterling, which I bound myself by the said marriage contract to pay to the heir of the marriage between me and my said wife, all in exact terms of the said marriage contract. *Fifth*, To make payment to my brother, the said John Gifford, and to my sister, Mrs Mary Gifford or Raleigh, widow of the late Reverend Doctor Alexander Raleigh, of the sums of £1000 each. I know that they do not need any pecuniary provision, and I make herein separate bequests to their children as aftermentioned, but they will accept of these sums from me as mere testimonies of my esteem and regard. *Sixth*, To pay, dispose of, invest, and apply the sum of £2500 to and for each of my nephews and nieces, who at present are ten in number, the children of my brother, the said John Gifford, and of my sister, the said Mrs Mary Gifford or Raleigh—that is to say, to each of Margaret Balmer Gifford or Scott, spouse of the said Andrew Scott; James Gifford, now in South Africa; the said Adam West Gifford; and Mary Jane Gifford or Croll, spouse of Andrew Usher Croll, Glasgow, the children of the said John Gifford; Catherine Anne Raleigh, residing in London; Alice Isabella Raleigh, now residing with me at Granton House; Jessie Raleigh, residing in London; the said Walter Alexander Raleigh; Ada Margaret Raleigh, and Agnes Crum Raleigh, both also residing in London, all children of the said Mrs Mary Gifford or Raleigh. Now my will is that my trustees shall hold for each of my said nephews and nieces who may survive me, and for their respective issue equally, the said sum of £2500 each in liferent, for their respective liferent uses allenarly, the issue of each nephew or niece taking the fee, and failing issue of each respective nephew or niece, the disposal of the fee being absolutely with the said respective nephews or nieces themselves; but declaring that if the trustees think proper, they may advance to any of my said nephews or nieces any sum not exceeding £1000; my meaning is that my said trustees shall hold the amount of the said legacies for behoof of my said nephews and nieces, and invest the same in heritable or personal property, or in the purchase of heritage, and pay the free income or produce thereof to my said nephews and nieces as an alimentary fund, exclusive of the *jus mariti* of husbands and of the diligence of creditors, at such times and in such sums as my trustees may think proper; and in case of the death of any of my said nephews and nieces, their respective children shall take their parent's share of the capital equally, and failing children they shall each have power to dispose of their shares of the capital at pleasure, and failing their doing so, it shall go to the survivors equally, share and share alike, and the issue of any predeceasing nephew or niece. And I would suggest to my said nephews and nieces, and each of them, that as these liferented legacies form, as it were, a family fund to secure against want, and I have therefore made them alimentary, and as it is intended to secure by means thereof a comfortable maintenance, so I think that if any of my said nephews or nieces are rich or comparatively rich, they may give up part or even the whole of their liferent to those who are poor or comparatively poor, so as to make the fund as useful as possible, but in all cases this is to be left to the pure good will and pleasure of each of my nephews and nieces themselves, and to their own feeling, without being dictated to by anybody or influenced otherwise than by their own sentiments of love and kindness. *Seventh*, In order to interest my son, the said Herbert James Gifford, in the said alimentary scheme and legacies, I direct my said trustees to set aside for him the sum of £2500 in addition to his other provisions, and to invest the said sum of £2500 along with and in the same way as the alimentary shares of his cousins, and to apply the interest in exactly the same way for his behoof, and I make the same suggestions in every way just as if he had been one of my nephews, and I destine his legacy so liferented in the same way. *Eighth*, I direct and appoint my said trustees to use and employ the sum of £40,000 as follows for behoof of my son, the said Herbert James Gifford, and his heirs and those substituted to him as aftermentioned—that is to say, my trustees shall apply the said sum of £40,000 in the purchase of lands and heritages of a permanent value, or of a value likely to increase either in one locality or in several localities within the United Kingdom or its islands, and shall entail the same, that is, they shall convey the lands and properties to purchases by settlement of strict entail in form of law to and in favour of the following series of disponees and heirs, that is to say, to and in favour of the said Herbert James Gifford, my son, in liferent for his liferent use allenarly during his lifetime, and after his death to the heirs male of his body, whom failing, the heirs female of his body, secluding heirs portioners, the eldest heir female for the time always exclusive of the others, whom failing, to the said Walter Alexander Raleigh, my nephew, for his liferent use allenarly during his lifetime, and after his death to the heirs male of his body, whom failing, the heirs female of his body, secluding heirs portioners, the eldest heir female for the time always exclusive of the others, whom failing, to the said Adam West Gifford, my nephew, in liferent for his liferent use allenarly during his lifetime, and after his death to the heirs male of his body, whom failing, to the heirs female of his body, secluding heirs portioners, the eldest heir female for the time always exclusive of the others, whom all failing, to my seven nieces above named, equally among them, share and share alike, and failing any of them by death, to her issue, each child taking, if more than one, an equal part of the mother's share, and to the survivors of my said nieces, and to their respective heirs, assignees, and successors whomsoever, thus terminating the entail; declaring that my said trustees shall have full discretion to fix when and where the lands shall be bought, or even to decide to keep the money invested on security for a series of years, if they shall think that preferable, or to buy to a greater extent than £40,000, borrowing the difference on the security of the purchase, and if there be on any of the lands so purchased a mansion house or mansion houses inhabited by the heir in possession for the time, then I suggest (but it is a mere suggestion) that it be made a kind of visiting place for my relatives, in some such manner as Granton House has been, so to promote good feeling among all. *Ninth*, I leave and bequeath all my household and garden furniture, and all my corporeal moveables, books, and chattels to my son, Herbert James Gifford, only suggesting that my brother, the said John Gifford, should have any article or articles he may choose, and that the said Walter Alexander Raleigh, Adam West Gifford, and Thomas Raleigh should each select say one hundred volumes from my books, not being drawing-room books or books of plates. *Tenth*, I direct my trustees to pay the following legacies:—To the Reverend William Skae, M.A., classical master, Edinburgh, £100; to the Reverend James Smith, minister of the Free Church, Davidson's Mains, £100; to the Reverend George Philip, Free Church minister, Saint John's, Edinburgh, £100; to the Reverend Walter Chalmers Smith, Free Church minister, Free High Church, Edinburgh, £100; to the Granton Literary Institute, Granton, the sum of £25 sterling; to Alexander Johnston, my gardener, the sum of £20; to Edward Dillon, my butler, the sum of £20; to each of my servants, including the said Alexander Johnston and Edward Dillon, who shall be in my service at the time of my death, the sum of £10, and also the sum of £1 for every complete year they have been in my service, declaring that the wife of my gardener, and the wife of my lodgekeeper, and my post-boy shall be reckoned in the number of my servants; to Margaret Malcolmson, who was nurse to my son, now a stewardess, the sum of £20, all which legacies shall be paid the first Whitsunday or Martinmas after my death, as also any other legacies which I may leave under my hand, declaring that whatever is signed by me shall be held as under my hand, whether holograph or not, declaring that while legacies payable under this tenth purpose are to be payable at the first Whitsunday or Martinmas after my death, all the other purposes of my trust settlements shall be prestable at the first Whitsunday or Martinmas that shall happen six months after my death. And I give to my trustees all the powers and privileges conferred on trustees by law and statute, including a power to name factors and law agents, either of their own number or of strangers, and in both cases with suitable remuneration, and for whom they shall not be answerable further than that they were habit and repute solvent at the time of appointment. And I declare the preceding ten purposes of this trust to be preferable, and I direct that these ten purposes be fulfilled in the first place before any others and before any residue of my estate, or any part thereof, is disposed of, and before any residue is ascertained or struck, declaring that it is only what may remain of my means and estate after the said ten purposes are fulfilled that I call herein the 'residue' of my estate, and out of which I direct the lectureships aftermentioned to be founded and endowed. And in regard that, in so far as I can at present see or anticipate, there will be a large 'residue' of my means and estate in the sense in which I have above explained the word, being that which remains after fulfilling the above ten purposes, and being of opinion that I am bound if there is a 'residue' as so explained, to employ it, or part of it, for the good of my fellow-men, and having considered how I may best do so, I direct the 'residue' to be disposed of as follows:—I having been for many years deeply and firmly convinced that the true knowledge of God, that is, of the Being, Nature, and Attributes of the Infinite, of the All, of the First and the Only Cause, that is, the One and Only Substance and Being, and the true and felt knowledge (not mere nominal

knowledge) of the relations of man and of the universe to
Him, and of the true foundations of all ethics and morals,
being, I say, convinced that this knowledge, when really
felt and acted on, is the means of man's highest well-being,
and the security of his upward progress, I have resolved,
from the 'residue' of my estate as aforesaid, to institute and
found, in connection, if possible, with the Scottish Universities, lectureships or classes for the promotion of the study
of said subjects, and for the teaching and diffusion of sound
views regarding them, among the whole population of
Scotland, Therefore, I direct and appoint my said trustees
from the 'residue' of my said estate, after fulfilling the said
ten preferable purposes, to pay the following sums, or to
assign and make over property of that value to the
following bodies in trust:—*First*, to the Senatus Academicus
of the University of Edinburgh, and failing them, by
declinature or otherwise, to the Dean and Faculty of
Advocates of the College of Justice of Scotland, the sum of
£25,000. *Second*, To the Senatus Academicus of the University of Glasgow, and failing them, by declinature or
otherwise, to the Faculty of Physicians and Surgeons of
Glasgow, the sum of £20,000. *Third*, To the Senatus
Academicus of the University of Aberdeen, whom failing,
by declinature or otherwise, to the Faculty of Advocates of
Aberdeen, the sum of £20,000. And *Fourth*, To the Senatus
Academicus of the University of St Andrews, whom
failing, by declinature or otherwise, to the Physicians and
Surgeons of St Andrews, and of the district twelve miles
round it, the sum of £15,000 sterling, amounting the said
four sums in all to the sum of £80,000 sterling; but said
bequests are made, and said sums are to be paid in trust
only for the following purpose, that is to say, for the
purpose of establishing in each of the four cities of
Edinburgh, Glasgow, Aberdeen, and St Andrews, a Lectureship or Popular Chair for 'Promoting, Advancing,
Teaching, and Diffusing the study of Natural Theology,' in
the widest sense of that term, in other words, 'The
Knowledge of God, the Infinite, the All, the First and Only
Cause, the One and the Sole Substance, the Sole Being, the
Sole Reality, and the Sole Existence, the Knowledge of His

Nature and Attributes, the Knowledge of the Relations which men and the whole universe bear to Him, the Knowledge of the Nature and Foundation of Ethics or Morals, and of all Obligations and Duties thence arising'. The Senatus Academicus in each of the four Universities, or the bodies substituted to them respectively, shall be the patrons of the several lectureships, and the administrators of the said respective endowments, and of the affairs of each lectureship in each city. I call them for shortness simply the 'patrons'. Now I leave all the details and arrangements of each lectureship in the hands and in the discretion of the 'patrons' respectively, who shall have full power from time to time to adjust and regulate the same in conformity as closely as possible to the following brief principles and directions which shall be binding on each and all of the 'patrons' as far as practicable and possible. I only indicate leading principles. *First*, The endowment or capital fund of each lectureship shall be preserved entire, and be invested securely upon or in the purchase of lands or heritages which are likely to continue of the same value, or increase in value, or in such other way as Statute may permit, merely the annual proceeds or interest shall be expended in maintaining the respective lectureships. *Second*, The 'patrons' may delay the institution of the lectureships, and may from time to time intermit the appointment of lecturers and the delivery of lectures for one or more years for the purpose of accumulating the income or enlarging capital. *Third*, The lecturers shall be appointed from time to time each for a period of only two years and no longer, but the same lecturer may be reappointed for other two periods of two years each, provided that no one person shall hold the office of lecturer in the same city for more than six years in all, it being desirable that the subject be promoted and illustrated by different minds. *Fourth*, The lecturers appointed shall be subjected to no test of any kind, and shall not be required to take any oath, or to emit or subscribe any declaration of belief, or to make any promise of any kind; they may be of any denomination whatever, or of no denomination at all (and many earnest and high-minded men prefer to belong to no ecclesiastical denomination);

they may be of any religion or way of thinking, or as is sometimes said, they may be of no religion, or they may be so-called sceptics or agnostics or freethinkers, provided only that the 'patrons' will use diligence to secure that they be able, reverent men, true thinkers, sincere lovers of and earnest inquirers after truth. *Fifth*, I wish the lecturers to treat their subject as a strictly natural science, the greatest of all possible sciences, indeed, in one sense, the only science, that of Infinite Being, without reference to or reliance upon any supposed special exceptional or so-called miraculous revelation. I wish it considered just as astronomy or chemistry is. I have intentionally indicated, in describing the subject of the lectures, the general aspect which personally I would expect the lectures to bear, but the lecturers shall be under no restraint whatever in their treatment of their theme; for example, they may freely discuss (and it may be well to do so) all questions about man's conceptions of God or the Infinite, their origin, nature, and truth, whether he can have any such concep-tions, whether God is under any or what limitations, and so on, as I am persuaded that nothing but good can result from free discussion. *Sixth*, The lectures shall be public and popular, that is, open not only to students of the Universi-ties, but to the whole community without matriculation, as I think that the subject should be studied and known by all, whether receiving University instruction or not. I think such knowledge, if real, lies at the root of all well-being. I suggest that the fee should be as small as is consistent with the due management of the lectureships, and the due appreciation of the lectures. Besides a general and popular audience, I advise that the lecturers also have a special class of students conducted in the usual way, and instructed by examination and thesis, written and oral. *Seventh*, as to the number of the lectures, much must be left to the discretion of the lecturer, I should think the subject cannot be treated even in abstract in less than twenty lectures, and they may be many times that number. *Eighth*, The 'patrons' if and when they see fit may make grants from the free income of the endowments for or towards the publication in a cheap form of any of the lectures, or any part thereof, or abstracts thereof, which they may think likely to be useful. *Ninth*, The 'patrons' respectively shall all annually submit their accounts to some one chartered accountant in Edinburgh, to be named from time to time by the Lord Ordinary on the Bills, whom failing, to the Accountant of the Court of Session, who shall prepare and certify a short abstract of the accounts and investments, to be recorded in the Books of Council and Session, or elsewhere, for preservation. And my desire and hope is that these lectureships and lectures may promote and advance among all classes of the community the true knowledge of Him Who is, and there is none and nothing besides Him, in Whom we live and move and have our being, and in Whom all things consist, and of man's real relationship to Him Whom truly to know is life everlasting. If the residue of my estate, in the sense before defined, should turn out insufficient to pay the whole sums above provided for the four lectureships (of which short-coming, however, I trust there is no danger), then each lectureship shall suffer a proportional diminution; and if, on the other hand, there is any surplus over and above the said sum of £80,000 sterling, it shall belong one-half to my son, the said Herbert James Gifford, in liferent, and to his issue other than the heirs of entail in fee, whom failing, to my unmarried nieces equally in fee; and the other half shall belong equally among my unmarried nieces. And I revoke all settlements and codicils previous to the date hereof if this receives effect, providing that any payments made to legatees during my life, shall be accounted as part payment of their provisions. And I consent to registration hereof for preservation, and I dispense with delivery hereof.—In witness whereof, these presents, written on this and the six preceding pages by the said Adam West Gifford, in so far as not written and filled in by my own hand, are, with the marginal notes on pages four and five (and the word 'secluding' on the eleventh line from top of page third, being written on an erasure), subscribed by me at Granton House, Edinburgh, this twenty-first day of August Eighteen hundred and eighty-five years, before these witnesses, James Foulis, Doctor of Medicine, residing in Heriot Row, Edinburgh, and John Campbell, cab driver, residing at No. 5 Mackenzie Place, Edinburgh.

AD. GIFFORD

James Foulis, M.D., Heriot Row,
    Edinburgh, *witness.*
John Campbell, cab driver,
    5, Mackenzie Place, *witness.*

RECOLLECTIONS
OF A BROTHER

ADAM GIFFORD

One of the Senators of the College
of Justice in Scotland

UNDER THE TITLE OF

LORD GIFFORD

BY HIS BROTHER

Printed for the use of the Family

NOTE

THESE recollections of my brother, Lord Gifford, are recorded by my sister and myself.

We are well aware that the record, containing no extraordinary or exciting incident, may seem trivial and commonplace. Still we know it tells the external life of one whom we loved much, and who was wise and good.

Besides most faithfully serving his own generation, he sought to benefit his country in time to come by founding the lectureships in Natural Theology.

These notes are printed *only* for the use of his relatives, their children, and their children's children, to supply some answer to the question, asked long after all his coevals have gone from earth, "Who was Lord Gifford?"

May these recollections stimulate some one to be wise and good as he was.

JOHN GIFFORD

Edinburgh, 1891.

RECOLLECTIONS OF A BROTHER,

AND OF HIS HOMES.

ADAM GIFFORD was born on February 29th, 1820, in Park Street, Edinburgh. There were afterwards in the family two other children, John and Mary.

His father, James Gifford, was the son of Adam Gifford, who was a manufacturer in leather. James, when he grew up, became a partner in the business, and carried it on after his father's death for the greater part of his life.

By industry and intelligence, he rose to a prominent place in his native city, as well as in the church to which he belonged. He became Treasurer and Master of the Merchant Company, a member of the Town Council of Edinburgh, and a governor of several charitable institutions. He was chosen an elder in the Antiburgher or Secession Church, and for many years was a diligent Sabbath-school teacher—this, too, at a time when Sabbath schools were not so common as they are now.

He had few opportunities in early life to acquire education, but, endowed with a clear perception, a sound judgment, and a natural power of language, he became an able and efficient man of business. He became more than this. His reading and thinking led him into regions beyond those in which most men live and move, and a certain far-sighted wisdom, touched with poetry and idealism, characterised his opinions. As a consequence, these were often in advance of his time; and his children have lived to see some ideas of his, which were regarded as utopian when he uttered them, secure a place in men's common thoughts.

He knew his Bible well, and loved it. There is no such book for developing the mind and heart.

My mother, Katherine Ann West, was the only daughter of John and Mary West. How shall I describe dear mother? She was younger than my father by six or seven years. Vigorous in body and mind, she was a most independent thinker—her thoughts ever more numerous than her words. She was not much taken up with the externals of life, but deeply impressed with its spiritual realities. This made her friends say "She was easy-going," and her economies in household management and decisions in practical life were carried through regardless of criticism.

Like her husband, she loved the Lord, and earnestly and constantly served Him.

My father had two brothers, John and Alexander—one older and one younger than he. John was a minister of the Secession Church, and had a congregation at Saltcoats, from the year 1800 till his resignation in 1811. Alexander was a solicitor in Edinburgh, and prospered in his business for many years. Father and he were very brotherly.

Mother had two step-sisters, Jean and Mary, daughters of her mother and her mother's second husband, Wm. Paterson. Jean married Mr James M'Laren, and had a large family of four sons and nine daughters—these cousins were our closest and most intimate friends of youth, as those of them who survive are of our advanced years. Mary married the Rev. William Lothian, a Congregational minister in St Andrews. Two of their children still survive.

For other relatives we must refer to the genealogical tree, only noticing other two cousins (Adam and Catherine), children of Alexander Gifford and his wife, Catherine More. They were both very dear to us, and grew up with us. They both died in early life of consumption,—Catherine in 1851, and Adam in 1853.

ARNISTON PLACE, No. 11, now called No. 25 Newington Road, is the first home of which my memory bears any record. I remember the "flitting" from Park Street, and the wonder and curiosity which the new house excited. It had a plot of grass in the front, and behind, a strip of garden ground. Father purchased this house, and found great delight in it and in the garden. He put up a summer-house, and a dove-cot, and with hammer and nails did many a little piece of work in and outside the house. It must have been in 1824 or 1825 that we came to this pleasant dwelling. The walls of the garden were clothed with fruit trees and currant bushes, and on them some cherries, pears, and ribston pippins ripened. There my brother's education and mine began under our mother's tuition. She had been a governess in the Rev. Dr Traill's family at Panbride, Forfarshire, and was thoroughly qualified to teach the elements of an English education. Adam and I were never at any elementary school.

I remember our writing lesson was at 7 o'clock, before breakfast; but the process of learning to read I do not remember,—it was so carried on that as we learned to speak we learned to read without knowing how.

Our dear sister Mary was born here in 1825, and no doubt our relation to her was a new element of education. In these early years I had (though very rarely) quarrels with Adam, and I remember it always ended in my crying for mother's help. He never was passionate, and only passively resisted my attacks.

The wee girl had no companions except her big brothers, four or five years older than she was, and I suspect we sometimes ran off to our games without her; for, whenever she saw a conference regarding some unknown project, she used to exclaim most emphatically, "Me too! Me too!"—thus early asserting woman's rights.

When Adam was eight and I about seven, we were placed under the care of Mr John Laurie, who kept a small school in West Nicolson Street for teaching Latin and Greek. He was a good man, but not a good teacher, and though we were there four or five years, I do not think we learned much. Adam learned better and more than I did. In the intervals of waiting, which were long at Mr Laurie's, as each class was called up in turn, Adam learned shorthand by himself—an acquirement of which in after years he made constant use.

About 1832 we became pupils of Mr Cunningham, who opened the Edinburgh Institution in Hill Street in that year. It might be said that a new era in education began there. Latin and Greek were retained, but French, German, Mathematics and English Literature were included, and boys were trained for life on a wider and more practical plan.

My brother was in higher classes than I, and became

really a good scholar. We ever retained a warm respect for
Mr Cunningham. He was an excellent man as well as a kind
and able teacher, and the school prospered.

My father left Nicolson Street Secession Church when
he came to Newington, and mother and he went to Rev.
Dr Gordon's, in Hope Park Chapel. I remember the pew
we sat in, but nothing else about the church. Some years
afterwards we went to Rev. Dr John Bruce's in the New
North Church, whose sermons mother enjoyed. Adam and
I went to his class for boys. He was succeeded by Rev. C. J.
Brown, from whose vigorous, impressive Scriptural teaching, we gained much. How much we never knew.

Our boyhood was spent in this home. My brother's
history in these days was not eventful. He shared in most of
our doings, but never led in them. There was a kind of
distance between him and even his playmates. The cousin
M'Larens were the most intimate, and David, about two
years older than Adam, was his frequent companion.

Saturday walks were a most important element of our
lives. Arthur's Seat, Blackford Burn, and subsequently
Portobello, were often visited. We made boats with our
pen-knives, and to launch them full-rigged on Blackford
Burn was an event of great interest. I remember a nice boat
of Adam's with a lugger sail, "The Earl Grey," suffering
under the stones thrown at it by some carter boys.
Moredun Mill, two miles out of Edinburgh on the Gil-
merton Road was a paradise for us. Mr Salmond, the
miller, a friend of father's, invited us on a Saturday now
and then, and we enjoyed it much, for there were the mill
and pond, a wood and a burn, besides a pony, and a garden
with gooseberries and currants, a world of delights to town
boys as we were.

Once a year father and some friends got up a pic-nic to
Habbies Howe in the Pentland Hills. We had only carts
with clean straw to carry us the ten miles, but it was
glorious in prospect and in execution.

The mates we were oftenest with were James and Hugh
Pillans, and the two Fergusons, Archie and Robert. On the
Saturdays many a mile we walked together with them—of
these four, Robert Ferguson has long been dead, the other

three still survive, with the honour and respect of their early playfellows, and of all who know them.

Even then my dear brother seemed to read more and think more than we did, and this led us in those early days to call him "the philosopher." Some of our social amusements he did not join in. We had a Society for asking and answering questions (these we printed in the form of a little catechism), and a "Picture Exhibition." To neither of these he contributed. He and I played chess a good deal when we were ten or twelve years old. We made with our penknives more than one set of chess men, but, when lessons became harder and life busier, chess as it took too much time was given up.

One other memory of Arniston Place may be recorded. I remember Miss Ann Traill staying with us and painting a portrait of Dr Gordon. The Doctor was throned in an arm-chair in the dining-room, with a bright red shawl of mother's thrown round him. Miss Traill afterwards joined the Church of Rome, and became one of the Sisters of Charity when they were established at Whitehouse Loan, Edinburgh, under the title of St Margaret's Convent.

Two scenes of our amusements may be sketched. At the top of our back garden on the other side of the wall was a piece of unoccupied ground. This was our frequent resort, and on the King's birthday, our Saturday halfpennies having been accumulated for weeks before, we had a small supply of gunpowder and some pieces of small artillery. We gathered sticks and got stones, made a "bonfire," roasted potatoes in the ashes, and were very jolly. Once I was sent over the wall to "borrow" a lump of coal from mother's cellar. When I got to the head of the garden, before throwing the coal over the wall I called out as a warning. One of the Fergusons misunderstood the call, and ran to the spot only to receive on his head the full force of the large piece of coal. It knocked him down, and we all, I especially, got a fright. This fortunately was the only result. The network of walls that enclosed the gardens of the neighbouring houses was a field of constant entertainment.

We made, like the cats, a regular walk round all the walls—they had a level copestone, and on it we enjoyed our freedom. The proprietors unfortunately objected to our presence, and sent the police after us.

This added zest to the enterprise, and we had barrel staves with a string attached to one end, which served as scaling ladders to enable us to reach the top of the wall easily and escape the officers.

One of the neighbouring houses was occupied by the notorious Dr Knox, who was associated with the murderers Burke and Hare. I remember well the evening when the mob assaulted his house, and smashed every pane of glass in his and the adjoining houses. Knox himself made his escape by these back garden walls.

No. 3 HILL SQUARE.—It must have been about 1835–6 that father bought this house and some property adjoining from his brother. Alexander Gifford had bought the Hill Square property for his house and office, and as he now wished to remove to St Andrew Square, he sold the whole to my father.

The Arniston Place house was sold at this time, and we unwillingly removed to No. 3 Hill Square.

The house was commodious enough, but the situation was confined, and we missed the fresh air of Newington.

However, we were now much busier. Adam had gone as an apprentice to Uncle, and was busy with law studies. He had entered the University and attended several classes. Our Saturday walks and games somehow ceased.

Father had his shop at No. 98 South Bridge, and still carried on his leather work. He made leather cases for hats, spectacles, and measuring lines, leather pipes for fire engines and breweries, and helmets for yeomanry. I helped in his book-keeping, marking measuring lines, and in other ways.

One day Mr John Macfie of the Sugar House, Canongate, saw me in the shop, and, turning to father, said, "Would your boy like to learn banking? I could get him into the National Bank of Scotland. I'm a Director there." I made no objections, so, with my Uncle's help, and a regular canvass by myself of all the Directors, on 25th April, 1836, I entered and was apprenticed to the National Bank of Scotland. I was hardly fifteen years of age.

Adam's life was now much more apart from mine. His heavy office work, the University studies, the Scots Law Debating Society filled up every hour. Then he read a great deal at night. All he did was done quietly and was never the subject of his talk, so that his work was not brought before us. He was often late of getting home at night, and family hours were early, evening prayers being at about 9.30. Supper and bed followed soon. Long after, Adam mentioned with gratitude that at this time mother gave him a pass-key, and never asked when he came in. He soon made himself useful to his Uncle, and learned his business thoroughly, until he became managing clerk in the office. He did everything systematically and perfectly, never grudging time or trouble.

One recreation on Duddingston Loch on the bright, cold winter days, he enjoyed. He became a good skater, and years afterwards joined the Skating Club. I remember going out with him, on the clear ice, at six o'clock in the morning, under the moonlight, to get a couple of hours skating—we had no other time. It was ever to be regretted that this was his only physical amusement. Had it been otherwise, and had riding, fishing, or golf got some of his hours in after days, his health and life might have been prolonged.

During these years we both became Sabbath-school teachers, and Adam taught for many years in Mr Ritchie's Heriot School, Cowgate. He taught and addressed the children most effectively. He also used to go on Sabbath forenoons to Dr Guthrie's Ragged School, to take a service with the poor children there.

His cousin Adam had been trained in his father's office for some years as a clerk.

Mr Alex. Gifford's business, though a good one, was not sufficient to be a source of income to both my brother and cousin, so, in the year 1848, the two Adams had a conference; my brother said to his cousin:—"You see there is not room for both you and me in this business. One of us must go out, and might perhaps pass as an advocate. Will you go or shall I?" Our cousin chose to remain, and my brother passed as an advocate in 1849.

I was married that year to my dear wife, Mary Usher. We went together to the Court of Session to see Adam pass as an advocate. He assumed the wig and gown, delivered a formal speech before the judges and took the oath of office. Thus his life work began. He had many mental qualities which fitted him for it. He had a strong, clear intellect, undisturbed by excess of emotion. He was able to take a wide and balanced survey of any subject. He had indomitable perseverance, patience to attend to details, and an excellent memory, well stored with general and professional information. All this made him an able advocate, and afterwards an impartial and wise judge.

He had other advantages when he started on this career. He was well known in conducting his uncle's business to many of the law agents, and his knowledge of the details of a solicitor's business was of much advantage to him in his new work.

Adam's first chambers were in Albany Street. I remember the door-plate with his name, but I do not think I was ever in his rooms.

We never liked our residence in Hill Square, and now, when Adam and I had left home, my father resolved to move to a house in Dublin Street, where an advocate's business could be carried on and the family could reside. It was No. 21, and they entered it, I think, in May 1851.

My father had retired from business years before this time, but he held the office of Treasurer to Trinity Hospital, an institution for the support of poor aged men and women, and to carry on this and the management of some house property, he retained an office at 105 South Bridge.

The Dublin Street house was in my brother's name, though father really upheld it—no doubt Adam contributed his share, but all his doings and his work were carried on so quietly we never heard of it. Indeed, since my marriage I was not in a position to learn much of these things. In 1851 our only sister was married to the Rev. Alex. Raleigh, a marriage which was a source of happiness and blessing to us all.

My father and mother, with Adam, removed again in May 1855. Adam bought the house No. 35 DRUMMOND

PLACE, and there, for years, he diligently and ably did the business that came to him. It came slowly, but his clients never left him; they soon learned the value of his work. He never would canvass for business. I remember once when I urged him to do so, he refused, saying playfully, "You know, John, if they don't employ me, it is their loss, not mine."

In August 1861 he and I went to Paris, and spent fourteen days very pleasantly.

He took no part in politics, although very decided in his Liberal views; and it was not till the year 1861, when he had attained considerable prominence in the Parliament House, and the Government could no longer pass him over, that he was appointed advocate-depute, and in 1865 Sheriff of Orkney and Shetland.

This latter office did not interfere with his work as an advocate. He appointed resident deputy-sheriffs, who heard the cases, and from whose decision an appeal could be made to him. Once or twice a year the principal Sheriff had to visit his County, and hold Courts. In the autumn of 1866 I went to Shetland with my brother. He hired a yacht at Lerwick, called "The Gem," of some thirty or forty tons, and we spent a very pleasant fortnight in sailing round and through among the islands. It was fine weather, and we had Deputy-Sheriff Muir and Mr Jas. D. Marwick (now Sir James) with us. I visited my friend, Mr John White, the Agent for the Union Bank at Lerwick at that time, and had many a ride over the moors before returning to Edinburgh.

The next event of importance in Adam's life was his marriage with Miss Maggie Elliot Pott.

Our Uncle Alexander had, in 1855, married Miss Jane Gray. She had been governess in the family of Mr James Pott, W.S., Albany Street, for a long time, and his wife on her deathbed, gave her charge of her two sons, James and George, and her only daughter, Maggie. After Miss Gray's marriage with Mr Alexander Gifford, Maggie Pott came to reside with her. It was an arrangement which suited all parties. Maggie was a bright, intelligent girl of sixteen or seventeen, and she brightened Uncle's home by her presence. The childless old man grew fond of her.

Yet, while my father lived, Adam never thought of bringing a new mistress to Drummond Place. Father's death took place in 1862—peacefully he had spent his last years: his strength was impaired, but not his clearness of mind. I had to go to Ireland that summer about a Bank Note robbery, and took my wife with me. Father and I walked together in the Drummond Place Gardens on the day I left. He said to me, "All my work is over, God has more than fulfilled all my wishes, and I am waiting his call." On the 27th July 1862, a telegram reached us while we were in Dublin, saying, "Father died this morning." He died in peace.

It was next year, 7th April 1863, that Adam's marriage with Miss Pott took place. Dear mother welcomed her warmly, and gave up her rule at Drummond Place to her new daughter. We all liked Adam's wife; she was so unselfish and kind, so clever and considerate.

The marriage was in Mr Alexander Gifford's house, and from that time our mother went to live with Mrs Raleigh in London, coming in the summer to visit Adam's home and mine.

My brother's home was a very happy one. Maggie's skill and sympathy brightened and soothed his few leisure hours, for his business had much increased, and he had secured a lucrative practice.

He and I had previously resumed the habit of having a walk or drive together every Saturday after noon. When the bank closed at one or two o'clock, I went to Drummond Place, and Adam pushed away his papers, and was always ready for our ramble. He had many acquaintances, but he never made any close friendships.

Herbert James, his first and only son, was born 12th March 1864. We lost our boy, John, 28th June of that year, of diphtheria.

Four happy years passed away over Adam's home. His boy grew strong and well, but during these years his wife's health slowly declined. All through 1867 her ever-wasting strength marked the months as they passed. Her husband watched over her with unceasing care, but her illness steadily increased. On the 7th of February 1868, a message came to me from him saying, "Come, dear Maggie is sinking." It was too true. When I saw on the pillow the pale, white face, and the bright eyes opening for a few seconds, to shed the light of affection and peace on her loved husband as he stood at her side, I felt that the look said "Farewell." She died that day, leaving him in sorrow too deep for expression. Little Herbert could not know then how great his loss was. Our mother came soon, and comforted the mourners as only a mother can—pouring out her warmest affection and most earnest prayers on and for the little motherless boy. All was done to keep in his memory some remembrance of her who loved him so dearly and left him so soon.

Unexpectedly, on 26th January 1870, Adam was appointed to a Judgeship in the Court of Session. As a Senator of the College of Justice he took his seat under the title of Lord Gifford. His father had predicted this elevation, yet we were surprised, as well as pleased when the appointment was made. He was only forty-nine—an early age at which to reach the bench.

Now our notes pass from Drummond Place to GRANTON HOUSE.—This house was taken in the end of 1870, and the removal to it took place in January 1871.

It was a fine old house, situated above the shore one and a half miles west of the Granton railway station. Built by President Hope of the Court of Session on land feued from the Duke of Buccleuch, the house stands on a bank some seventy feet above the sea, and commands a fine view north, west, and east. Above thirty acres are attached to the house, and a ring of trees shelter and shut it in. There were two or three small parks, a good old-fashioned garden and stabling, etc., included in the property.

Sundry additions had been made to the house, and it had accommodation for a large establishment.

Granton House was a happy meeting-place. Here the various branches of the family were gathered from time to time under the kind and generous hospitality of my brother.

Till the time of her death in December 1873, our mother made it her home, and found a peaceful resting-place in it, while she studied and struggled to do her utmost for the comfort and welfare of Adam and for Herbert, whose motherless condition touched her heart.

Subsequently, Lord Gifford had the good fortune to have successively as his housekeepers and companions his two dear nieces, Katy and Alice Raleigh. Alice's loving care was with him all through his long illness, and she was at his side when he breathed his last.

As a Judge, Lord Gifford required a carriage to take him to and from the Court, but often the grey horses carried a happy party of children; for, in his kindness, Lord Gifford made his home a veritable holiday house for my sister's children and mine. Many delights were there. The freedom of the woods, the sea-bathing, the wonders of the shore, the fruits and flowers of the garden, always freely given, these things were the foundation on which many a superstructure of childish bliss was built, to be remembered with moist eyes in after days.

Herbert's first pony, Donald, a sturdy Shetlander, shaggy and wilful, was an important member of the family. After him came a larger animal Fairy,—these were the gifts of his uncle, Mr George Pott, and were a constant source of pleasure. There were dogs too, Jet, Trap, Charlie, and Faust, distinct in their several characters and ways, and not to be forgotten.

The two servants longest in Lord Gifford's employ were Alex. Johnston, the gardener—a shrewd, useful, and faithful man—and Dillon, the butler, an Irishman than whom none could be more good-natured and thoroughly attached to his master.

Johnston was lord of his own domain, and a kind of warfare was often carried on with much zest between him and the boys—(Herbert, Walter Raleigh, and my two sons James and Adam). They could not always accept his verdict as to when gooseberries or cherries were ripe, or which plots of currant bushes or strawberries were to be kept sacred for jam, or which fences were not to be climbed upon.

As for Dillon—his good nature sometimes tempted to extreme measures the same mischievous hands. Once, at least, he was found tied hand and foot in his own pantry, and it is said his cupboards were unaccountably short of raisins and nuts at that very time. But under all such trials, his patience, good nature, and ready Irish wit never forsook him.

The incidents to be recorded now are few. In 1872, my brother complained of a numbness in his right leg which nothing could remove, and which ultimately made him lame, dragging that limb when he walked. There is no doubt that this was the first approach of the paralysis that afterwards became more masterful, and at last extinguished his vital powers. Still, at this time, it never affected his activity of mind or body—both were able for full work.

Dear mother died on Christmas Eve in 1873. She was as well as usual till three days before her death. Her three children were by her side, and saw her close her eyes and fall asleep in Christ. How good and how dear she was, and how much she was missed! She was 87 years old when she died.

About the year 1880 my brother's lameness had much increased, and he walked more feebly—indeed, more than once, he fell from sudden failure of his limbs. On New Year's Day, 1881, he came to us at 4 Marchmont Terrace, dined with us, and stayed overnight, going to Court next day. That day, the 2nd of January, a messenger came to me to the bank, at four o'clock, saying that Lord Gifford had been seized with illness at the Court. I went at once, and found him sitting in one of the retiring rooms with his clerk, Mr Henderson, and Mr David Duncan, a good friend of our family. A cab was got, and with difficulty my dear brother and I reached Granton House.

He had sat on the Bench and heard the cases with his usual care, till he found he could not move from his seat. He gave no sign, but waited nearly half-an-hour till the Court rose, and then sent for assistance to his clerk, who got Mr Duncan. They found his limbs quite powerless, and sought medical help at once.

He never walked again, nor again entered the Court.

The best medical advice could do nothing. It was a severe shock of paralysis. His limbs and his right hand were powerless, but his head and heart were clear and calm. He knew exactly what had happened, and he was most grateful that God had left him his mind untouched.

After waiting a few weeks, and finding his recovery partial and slow, he resigned his Judgeship, and retired after twelve years' service. Government kindly gave him the usual pension. The sincere regret and the affectionate esteem of his fellow-Judges, and of those associated with him in his profession, went with him as he closed his legal career.

The history of the long six years which he spent almost prostrate, fighting with his deadly disease, can be soon told. His right arm being paralysed, he learned to write with his left hand till his other was restored.

The disease, after six months of partial recovery, with a violent shock attacked the left side, and made him still more powerless. His sister, Mrs Raleigh, was in the house at the time of the seizure, and was called to come to his room at four o'clock on a July morning. Entering softly, and with a troubled heart, she can never forget his calm look, and the words with which he greeted her,—

"*This is a march on the citadel.*"

That same day, when we were still uncertain as to the issue of the attack, I said, standing by his bed, and thinking how vain was all human help, "*In Him* we live and move and have our being." He looked up to me, and said slowly, "Yes, and *in Him we die.*" He did not die then, but lived five years longer, till patience had its perfect work.

At various intervals he experienced attacks of a slight but similar nature, all of which undermined his naturally vigorous vitality. Indeed it was considered most wonderful that he could sustain and recover from so many attacks.

Two men waited on him day and night to supply all his wants; and all through this weary time, besides the constant care of Herbert and Alice, my sister often came from London, and stayed for weeks or months; and every week at least, I spent hours at his bedside.

Nothing could exceed the wise and careful attention of his doctor, Dr Foulis, during these years. Regulation of the diet and of the daily life was all that could be done. He was placed in the wheel-chair in the afternoon, and, if the weather was fine, he was taken through the grounds, and then a cup of tea and biscuits were served under the elm or under the roses. He enjoyed this change, and talked cheerily with any of us who happened to be there at the time. He was wheeled to the dining room if the weather was bad. Many of his friends saw him, and had a pleasant though brief talk with him. The great advantage of having a country house and fresh air was felt in these circumstances.

My brother's patience under his heavy trial was wonderful and most touching; words he spoke from time to time revealed the source of his resignation. Some of them I recall, such as—"I have often wished for leisure to read and to think, now I have it,"—"I think I have seen more clearly many things about God since I have been laid aside; in the night I often can't sleep, and I follow out new trains of thought about Him,"—"I am very helpless, but I don't wish it to be otherwise; it is best as it is." His doctor for a time thought it possible that he might recover so far as to be able to walk with the help of crutches, and said so. He himself never thought it likely. "No," he said to his sister, "I will never walk again, but it doesn't matter. I need no crutches; there are *wings* ready for me to bear me home to God."

"To be happier or wiser, that just means to have *more of God.*" The emphasis he laid on these three last words cannot be conveyed on paper.

Sometimes his fertile fancy would lead him to make very quaint remarks. Once, after a sleepless night, of which he had many, he said to his sister,—"I had a bitter quarrel with my body last night, I put the blame of all I have to bear on *it*. But I was very careful to use none but Scripture language in abusing it. I called it 'this vile body,' 'the body of this death,' 'this corruptible,' the tabernacle, in which 'I groan, being burdened.' So all I said was true and reasonable."

In bed, in a room facing south, and looking out on lawn and trees, he was supported with high pillows, and had his writing materials, papers and books all round him. He was always occupied and interested, till the last year of his life, when his illness increased, and he read less, and looked more weary. There were many conversations on the highest of all subjects in that quiet room. Shall we ever forget them? The reticence of other years was gone, he spoke freely of what he thought, and most often his thoughts were of God. He used to say, "He is infinite, how can our finite minds grasp His Being? but it is not wrong to go on in our thinking as far as we can."

Speaking of doing good to others, he used to say, "There is one person we can always try to make better, and that is ourselves."

One day he said to me, "John, I got a terrible fright last night." "What frightened you?" I asked. "Oh, I discovered that I was beginning to love money!" Perhaps there is more cause for alarm on this ground, in many lives, than is at all realised.

Very pathetic it was to see him making cheerfully the best of what was left to him, never uttering a murmuring word, never regretting lost strength, but staying his heart calmly on the love and wisdom of his Father in heaven.

About a year before his father's death, Herbert went to London to prosecute his business as a Civil Engineer, as apprentice to Messrs Barry & Brunell. He had long been kept at home for his father's sake, but now it was felt he must go.

During that year the paralysis had tightened its hold and affected the internal functions more than before. My brother felt weaker, and could not think or speak as he used to do. He felt this, and often said that he wished to be done with his frail, useless body for ever.

About the middle of January 1887, he was more depressed and feebler. The doctor was anxious about him. I was at Granton House on Wednesday 19th January; he could speak little, and I was alarmed. However, I went home, Alice promising to wire any change. On Thursday, 20th January, a message came, "Uncle is worse, come." I drove down and found him very feeble. He knew me well, and smiling said, "I cannot speak;" that was about five o'clock. The oppression increased, and we could not understand his attempts to tell his wants.

Dr Foulis came about 7 o'clock, and told us Lord

Gifford would not see next morning. He had so rapidly sunk during the last hours that I said, "Doctor, stay a little; he will not live an hour." He stayed.

We gathered around him—my wife, Alice, my son Adam, and myself, and watched his heavy, feeble breathing, till at last Dr Foulis said, "Now it is over." "Is it indeed?" I exclaimed, for he seemed quieter and calmer than ever. I touched his hand—kissed his cold brow. He was gone. My dear brother was at home with his God. He died about nine o'clock on the evening of the 20th January 1887.

Herbert, unfortunately, though he travelled all night, did not arrive till next morning, and Mrs Raleigh was also too late to see her loved brother.

His death left not only my sister and myself without a brother, but took from us one of the dearest, most generous and noblest friends we ever had. None knew Adam as we did.

After providing for his son, and giving legacies to his nieces and nephews and dependants, his fortune, gained entirely by his own hand and brain, was so ample that he gave £80,000 to the four Universities of Scotland to found lectureships on Natural Theology. To the University of Edinburgh he gave £25,000; to those of Glasgow and Aberdeen, £20,000 each; and to St Andrews, £15,000.

The conditions and regulations of these lectureships were carefully and thoroughly detailed, to secure what was the earnest desire of the donor—the highest welfare of his fellow-men, by leading them to the knowledge of God.

It will surprise his friends to know that his heart never was entirely with his profession. With the technicalities and verbalism of law he had no sympathy, nor with the petty squabbles of men, to decide which he was obliged to give his close attention. The only region of law in which he could freely breathe was that in which are found the principles of true and unchanging justice. He was an equity lawyer, and in any case where he could apply these principles, he swept precedent and word-splitting aside and fearlessly did the right. He once said to me, "You are well off, John; when you lock your safe your mind and thoughts are free and fresh, but all last night and all this day I have had to investigate and make up my mind on a wretched, paltry dispute between two unreasonable men about a trifle."

He sought higher subjects of thought and higher enjoyments.

The remarkable fact was that, notwithstanding that his taste led him into fields other than his work, he yet did it so well.

Nothing distinguished him more than his fixed habit of doing everything he put his hand to most perfectly. He read his cases, mastered all the minute details, thought over them, arranged his arguments, or wrote his interlocutor with the utmost care. A case regarding the modes of measuring the tonnage of a ship once came before him. One of the parties told me that Lord Gifford drove down to Leith, sought out the vessel and its owner, and was led over the points in dispute that he might give an intelligent and just decision.

As an Advocate, he had much popular ability. Not naturally in the least impulsive, he knew the power of impassioned declamation over a jury or over a public meeting, and most fervently could he declaim. Other two qualities aided his popularity—his unfailing urbanity and the lucidity of his speech. None ever complained that Lord Gifford treated them with impatience, and none who gave any attention to his words could fail to understand them. An agent who lost his case said, "Mr Edward Gordon had stated our side, and I thought we were pretty safe. Your brother rose to reply, and, passing his hand through his long flowing soft hair, shook out his mane, and, like a lion, tore our case and our arguments to pieces. I felt utterly lost."

My brother's memory for things and words was most tenacious. He soon forgot his cases when they were over, but never till then. The amount of fine poetry he could repeat till his dying day was a source of pleasure and surprise to those who heard him.

His work as a Judge was most valuable; it was never careless or imperfect. He could see through each case and seize its points at once, and announce his decision.

In Commercial litigation his judgment was much sought, and gave general satisfaction. This was due in some measure to his fearless application of equity in guiding his decisions. Merchants prefer commonsense to law.

He refused to act as a Criminal Judge. I believe pity for the poor criminals, and a deep conviction that the wrong-doers had generally been deeply wronged, made him most unwilling to be their judge.

My brother's life and his enjoyments were found in intellectual pursuits.

He read much, and read on every subject. In his youth he wrote volumes of notes, where all his reading was gathered under its subjects, and these arranged alphabetically.

Every valuable fact or beautiful verse was indexed up under its leading word and thought. This made his mind a similar record, where, duly classified and easily found, all the treasures of his reading were preserved.

He read with his mind fully awake, and, as he marked each book he read, so every memorable thing was marked in his mind. While he read the records of the mighty thinkers of olden times in Latin, French, or German, and knew something of most of them in science and philosophy, he was fully abreast with the most recent thought.

Poetry was his favourite study and recreation. He always said that the highest and best thoughts expressed in the most suitable and beautiful words were to be found there, and he acted on this conviction, reading, criticising, and remembering the best of every poet's work as it passed under his eye. His notebooks were full of extracted beauties; and he could illustrate by poetical quotations almost any subject. Unfortunately they are written in shorthand.

When he resigned his office of Judge, he resigned his connection with law, ceased to read or think about it, and parted with some of his legal library.

His mind became more and more absorbed in Philosophy and Theology or rather Philosophic Theology. He had all his faculties during the first years of his illness, and he had ample leisure to employ them. They were largely engaged in the highest and most difficult problems of God's nature and man's relation to Him. He studied and admired Spinoza, yet always denied that he himself was a Pantheist, marking the distinction thus: "Spinoza holds that everything is God. I hold that God is everything; if I were to assume a name descriptive of my belief, I should be called a Theopanist." Thus he held that "force," "substance," "being," itself must be God, quoting many a text to show that the Bible agreed with his view, such as:—"I am," implying that besides God nothing was; "In whom we live and move and have our being." The 17th Chapter of John's Gospel was often referred to as declaring the unity of God with His creatures.

He sided with Bishop Berkeley in the doctrine of the superior evidence for the existence of mind compared with what we have for the existence of matter, and had no sympathy with materialism. He seemed sometimes to wish he had strength to contribute his thoughts, to counteract the prevailing materialistic philosophy of our day.

The Bible he knew well, and studied much, though he did not hold the doctrine of a verbal inspiration. He ever sought and found in it the highest and purest thoughts this world contains. The Gospel of John was more in harmony with his mind than the Pauline writings.

He loved clear, definite thought. Of Arnold's "Literature and Dogma," he said, "Well, 'literature' means undefined mysticism, 'dogma' defined ideas; all my sympathy is with the latter."

Indeed, often his attempts to define seemed to be applied to subjects too high for man's faculties to comprehend.

His favourite definition of the creature was "a part of the Infinite," for, he said the Infinite cannot be infinite if it does not include everything. He treated man's consciousness of personality and the testimony of his intuitions with little reverence, holding God and God's infinite existence as all and in all, overlooking that our knowledge of God, however imperfect, can only rest on our knowledge of ourselves. The terms of his will, in founding the lectureships of Natural Theology, illustrate this characteristic of his mind.

My brother's attitude towards God was most trustful, reverent and obedient. He had perfect confidence in God's goodness, and built his optimism on that foundation. During all his years of suffering and weariness not only did he never once complain, but often said, "It could not be better."

A strong sense of justice pervaded all his dealings with his fellow-men; carefully he gave every one his due. He was generous. The share of our father's estate which fell to him he never touched but handed it over to my sister and myself. He gave to me at another time the house at No 4 Lower Joppa, a present my children and their children enjoyed many a summer day.

Those who gathered round him at Granton House, his nephews and nieces, will never forget his kindness, nor find again such a generous and noble friend.

It was strange that, with such an admiration for beauty in the abstract, and as it existed in expressed thought, my brother had no enthusiasm for fine architecture, for beautiful painting, or for flowers.

Enriched as his mind was with such varied treasures, possessed with such clear and definite views on most important truth, and directed especially to Philosophic Theology, it was often regretted that his thoughts were not embodied in a book. Had his strength been prolonged he might have done so, but he has left nothing for publication.

Only in one direction has he left permanent traces of his thought. During his services as a Judge, he most willingly became a lecturer at many of the Literary and Philosophical Institutions of Edinburgh, and other towns of Scotland. On winter evenings he often travelled far to deliver carefully-studied lectures on such themes as The Life of St Bernard, The Avatars of Vishnoo, The Chemistry of Dust, The Foundations of Law, The Poetry of Adelaide Proctor, of Mrs Browning, Writings of Erasmus, Darwin, Emerson, or Parker, What is Substance? What is Force?

The productions were thoroughly thought out and richly adorned by a mind endowed with no ordinary amount of energy and beauty. A selection of these has been printed for private friends by his niece, Alice, and his son, Herbert.

His body was buried in the Old Calton Cemetery, where the dust of his wife, his father, and mother lie. The grave is close to the eastern wall of the burying-ground.

Selections from
LECTURES

DELIVERED ON VARIOUS OCCASIONS

BY

ADAM GIFFORD

The miscellaneous lectures from which these are a selection were given from time to time by request, on very various occasions and to greatly differing audiences. Their preparation was a great pleasure to the lecturer, the subjects being chosen by himself; but as they were almost all given during winter sessions, they were of necessity sometimes hurriedly, although never carelessly prepared. We have given them exactly as they are jotted down in his note-books, so far as that is possible, and have made no attempt to fill up the occasional gaps and deficiencies which were left to be supplied at the time of delivery.

They were in no case meant for publication, and we print a few of them now, only for his friends. To those who heard them delivered they may be additionally endeared by the recollection of the manifold characteristics of voice and gesture which were as peculiar to himself as his style.

ALICE RALEIGH
HERBERT JAMES GIFFORD

June 1889.

CONTENTS

I

RALPH WALDO EMERSON

Delivered in the City Hall, Glasgow.
November 1872

Twenty five years ago I heard Mr. Emerson deliver four lectures in Edinburgh. I had previously read his two series of Essays, read them with a fresh and startled admiration which, alas! is almost peculiar to the young;—and although his personal appearance was far from impressive, I listened to him with a youthful and an overflowing enthusiasm. That enthusiasm, Ladies and Gentlemen, *I still feel*. I rejoice to think that my early admiration was not misplaced. Time with his ruthless mace has shattered many idols of a fond but false worship. But let us thank God if we were not wholly idolators, if any of our youthful delights are delightful still, if some of the morning colours are unfaded, and part of its fine gold undimmed. I at least can gratefully rejoice to confirm my early verdict, and I think I can give my deliberate opinion, that, with perhaps three or four exceptions, there now lives no greater English writer than *Ralph Waldo Emerson*.

★   ★   ★

Emerson is not distinctively a religious writer, that is to say he does not profess to teach or to enforce religion, but his tone is eminently religious. The truth is, that although in education and elsewhere we may try to separate secular from sacred, and provide time-tables and conscience clauses and so on, religion will not be separated from anything whatever! It will penetrate every cranny and pervade every space, and it will flow around and through every subject and every substance like electricity. You cannot produce and you cannot maintain religious vacuum, and if you could, even secularism would die in it.

It is very difficult to gather from any of Emerson's writings what are his precise religious beliefs. He nowhere announces them, and it is only from scattered hints and implications that an approximation can be reached. He is still claimed as a Unitarian, although probably his true position is rather that of a philosophic Theist. I imagine he would not classify himself as either a Unitarian or a Trinitarian or a Polytheist; but that he would rather stand along with such men as his great contemporary Theodore Parker, who thought that *one* and *three* and many were just man's arithmetic of Deity, modes of human reckoning, finite aspects which can only have a figurative application to the Infinite. I gather also that he rather inclines to the higher or subjective pantheism; but he will not limit, and he cannot define. Before all such questions he stands uncovered and reverently silent. No proud denial, no cynic scoff, no heartless sneer escapes him; and without a theory of the universe he clings to its moral meaning. I believe he seems to say that the universe exists hospitably for the weal of souls. "I will bate no jot of heart or of hope though I cannot see the end of transgression. I know that there is a permanent behind everything that is mutable and fleeting; and though abyss open under abyss, and opinion displace opinion, all are contained in the Eternal Cause."

Is one who occupies this position to be blamed? The thoughtful and magnanimous will not say so. I cannot condemn that wise and humble scepticism, which, while reverently waiting and enquiring, refuses to say what it does not think, or to profess a belief which it does not feel. Let us all be patient and wait. To the upright, here or hereafter, light will arise; and meantime let us rejoice in every high and holy aspiration, and sympathise in every effort to elevate the character and improve the condition of man.

★   ★   ★

II

ATTENTION, AS AN INSTRUMENT OF SELF CULTURE.

Delivered before the Greenock Philosophical Society.
November 1874.

I think and speak to-night of the Greenock Philosophical Society solely as a means of *mental culture*; as an Institute which may tend or contribute to our mental improvement; and which, if rightly used, may make us wiser, and better, and more beautiful, (and that is really the same thing, for beauty is but the efflorescence and the source of goodness) wiser and better and more beautiful than we were before.

But even this is far too wide a subject for our lecture of to-night; and I think it will be better if we confine ourselves to a practical notice of *one single instrument* by the right use of which the culture I have spoken of may be made ours, and you and I and all of us may sensibly and appreciably, lecture after lecture, and session after session, become less and less *wild* and more and more *cultivated* men and women, bourgeoning into greenness, blossoming into the brightness, and bearing at last the purple fruitage which make glad the gardens of immortality!

Now the instrument of culture which I have selected as the topic of this Introductory Lecture is *attention*, "Attention as an instrument of self culture:" and if you and I can but grasp and carry away and keep with us some notion of the nature and of the use and of the mighty power of this instrument, my purpose will be fully answered. It will not be lost time however, if I remind you just in a few sentences what the culture is at which you are to aim.

★   ★   ★

The third kind of education is that which a man consciously and voluntarily gives himself, or to which he deliberately and intentionally exposes himself, in order that he may be moulded and changed and modified thereby. This I call *self education*, or *self culture*. It is that wonderful, most marvellous, most stupendous power given to a man, given to every man, given to each of us; consciously, deliberately to change his own nature, to make himself by his own act a different creature from what he was before.

★   ★   ★

It is a power peculiar to man. The plants and the animals around us are, equally with ourselves, sometimes even more than we, liable to hereditary or external change, the subjects of ancestral or of outward influence and culture. They as well as we are what they were born and what they have been made. But to us alone has it been given to make our own future, to say with deliberate choice and almost perfect foresight what manner of creatures we shall become, what nature we shall assume, what faculties we shall wield and perfect, and how it shall be with us and with our descendants in the long long ages which are to come. For, again observe, that this tremendous power of self culture does not determine the direction in which it is to go. It may lead upward, yonder; or downward, thither; and may issue (and I am not at all speaking theologically, but only scientifically), and may issue in the angel or the fiend.

★   ★   ★

I now limit myself to-night to *one* instrument of self culture, and that is the power of concentrating our minds on any subject or part of a subject we please. It is called *"Attention."*

★   ★   ★

By "attention" I mean *that power or that act of the mind by which it detains, or holds for inspection, any perception or conception, that is, any thought, to the exclusion of all others.* I am not going to enter upon, or even notice metaphysical speculations on the subject; however curious and interesting. They are endless, and my purpose to-night is not speculative but practical. It is enough that there is such a power, and such an act of the mind, by which it can hold a thought or an idea, and look at it alone, regarding and thinking of nothing else for the time. The exclusive occupation of the mind for a certain time, with one thought, one idea, one perception or conception only, is attention. By "perception" I mean any thing or any idea perceived either through the senses or by reflection, that is, by the internal powers of the mind. By "conception" I mean any thought or idea formed in the mind by an act of memory or imagination.

Now there is such a thing and such a power as *attention*.

★   ★   ★

Every one knows and acts upon this. The lecturer or the clergyman begins,—"Give me your attention!" Neither he nor you doubts but that you can give him your attention, if you please. "Attention!" cries the captain or the adjutant to the company of soldiers, and not a man of them but feels he can obey, and stands erect and ready for the order that is to follow. I think it may be said that none of our mental powers or faculties are so completely subject to the will, as attention is. In one sense indeed, and in a very important sense, it is the only faculty which is directly, purely, and entirely at our command and at our choice. We cannot hope or fear or believe or trust or enjoy what we please or what we would; but must use other and indirect means to bring about these states and conditions; but we can always attend to whatever we choose. If we are not responsible for our creeds we are at all events responsible for our studies. We may not command what we are to see, but we can at least command the eye to open and the mind to observe; and greater freedom than this we do not, we ought not, to desire.

In very truth, the power and freedom of will to attend to whatever we choose is the very highest power and the very noblest freedom which can be conferred upon a finite being. It is a higher power, a nobler freedom, than would be the power to create, absolutely to create, whatever we chose; for our creations could only be the poor reflections of our own littleness. But the power to contemplate what we choose lays before us, to make it our own, the limitless creation of God. The infinite fullness of the Godhead is unfolded to us, and we are invited to choose and expatiate in any department of the Infinite. Glory then, O man, in this thy wondrous liberty! Behold and see the works of the Lord! Come and see that God is Good!

★ ★ ★

Nature, or nature's great Author, while giving entire freedom and vast power to the human will, seldom trusts to its action alone to secure man's well-being. There are always other precautions taken, other and self-acting machinery brought into play, to secure the end though the will should fail to act. For example, our taking necessary food and drink is a voluntary act, it depends on our will what and when we shall eat and drink; but alas for us if there were nothing else to secure our nourishment! It is not left to our mere will. Nature has taken care to provide the pangs of hunger and thirst to drive us, and all the pleasures of taste to draw us, to take what is required for the sustenance of our bodies. And just so with our minds. Attention is the act of the *mind feeding*, so to speak; and although it is made entirely subject to the will, yet when the will is dormant or forgets to act, the attention is secured and stimulated by many a passion.

We naturally and necessarily attend to what we dread or fear; we watch that we may shun or escape it. Not less necessary is the eager look with which we regard the objects of love, of desire and of hope; and it needs no effort of will to make the eye strain to see and the ear keen to hear the distant indications of the longed-for blessing. So it is with many other emotions of our nature which I cannot even stop to name. For this purpose alone, (to secure attention when the will fails to act), it would seem that the passion or emotion of *curiosity* has been implanted in our minds, the desire to know simply for the sake of the knowledge itself: a passion which, however often abused, and however often made ridiculous, is yet, in itself, and in its radical nature, one of the very noblest of which man is susceptible. Judge nothing from its abuse! Think well, and perhaps you will find that it is curiosity which distinguishes man from brute and the philosopher from the clown.

★ ★ ★

Let attention only be yours, attention ever ready at our

command and docile to our wishes, attention awakened by pure desires and stimulated by noble emotions, attention intense and keen, dwelling upon elevating objects and ideas, reiterated upon the good, and the beautiful and the true, till these and these alone are loved and honoured; let such attention be daily and hourly practised, and we shall forthwith become sensible of daily and hourly growth. Our spirit will develop its spiritual wings, higher and nobler regions will become accessible to us, every week will add whole provinces to our government and every year will make new dominions tributary to our crown. Up and ever up this glorious future, we shall find in death only the opening of new worlds and the accession of fresh powers; and endowed with an unending existence we shall rejoice that there is spread for our enjoyment a universe infinite and divine.

III

SAINT BERNARD OF CLAIRVAUX

Delivered before the Morningside Literary Institute
February 1875.

The middle ages! What strange scenes and pictures do not the words recall? The fortalice of the half savage Baron and the mean huts of his degraded serfs. The proud pomp and spiritual power of the haughty churchman, before which the strength of kings, and the might of feudalism was fain to kneel. The chivalry of Europe drained time after time to furnish forth the armies of the Crusaders. Religious excitements and revivals passing like prairie fires over Europe, and compared with which modern revivals, even the wildest, seem but the coldest marsh gleams. Strange and terrible diseases and epidemics, and plagues both bodily and mental, that mowed down millions as with the scythe of destruction. The spotted plague and the black death and the sweating sickness. The dancing mania, the barking mania. The werewolf and the ghoul. Strange mystical schools of Philosophy exciting popular admiration and enthusiasm to us unexampled and inexplicable. And below all, the swelling and the heaving of the slow but advancing tide which even yet is bearing us upon its crest.

★   ★   ★

Undoubtedly sincere in all this course of conduct, I mean all through his frightful austerities, I think it is not possible, even when we condemn them, to withhold our tribute of admiration. Here at least is a man who believes in the unseen, and acts out his belief unflinchingly. No sham, no hypocrite, no simulacrum he! Is the body to be kept under? He tramples on it. Is a sensibility to be repressed? He strangles it. Is a passion to be subdued? By frost or by fire he will exterminate it. It is said that when he felt passion rising he walked into the cold marsh pool up to his ears and stood there till he was almost dead. Think of that: this man means victory, and gained it; and over and over again his determined struggle nearly cost him his life. I venerate such single-minded dauntless energy and self-sacrifice, and I almost willingly forget that it was mistaken. And do we not find this very quality to be the root and foundation quality of all greatness? I ask not, I almost care not, what a man's convictions may be; but I demand,—Does he work them out, fearlessly, unfalteringly, to the very end, however bitter that end may be? There is goodness in such a man, in the very depths of his delusions; for he is a man, a living will, and not a mirage and a shadow. But again, Bernard's asceticism and austerities were not so to speak mere selfish acts, ending on himself as secluded from the world. They were not the mere formalities of the solitary and almost mindless hermit, muttering and moping in semi-idiocy before his crucifix and his scull. Far, far different. They had all relation to his fellow men. Every fibre of him throbbed with sympathy, and every nerve trembled and thrilled to influence and to draw his neighbour: and truly the power and the influence went forth! Perhaps there never was a man who had a greater or more powerful *personal influence* than this Bernard. I am not speaking just now of his preaching, although of course his personal influence was felt in all his preaching. I mean simply the effect which his presence or address produced on all who came near him. His will or his attraction was predominant and irresistible. At the glance of his eye, at the wave of his hand, his enemies wheeled round and joined the ranks of his retainers, as if they had heard the mighty "follow me" of a greater than Saint Bernard.

★   ★   ★

But the secret of his preaching must have been the earnestness of his manner, or rather the intense and burning earnestness of his soul. In this connection, it is instructive to learn that the effect of his preaching was not less but often greater when he was preaching in a language which his audience did not understand. The truth is that in all ages, men, the common run and bulk of men, are far more led and swayed by their feelings and habits and emotions than by their understandings. It is not he who sees the highest truth, but he who touches the deepest chord of feeling that can bend the multitude to his will: and in Bernard we must simply recognise another of the masters of the human lyre, skilled to play upon its thousand strings.

★   ★   ★

A few words now on the miracles of Saint Bernard. For *he did work miracles*! manifold, varied and numerous. To doubt it is to be an unbeliever and a scoffer. There exist books on his miracles, attested by scores of eye witnesses, whose testimony nothing but judicial blindness can withstand. (One of these books is a very curious diary, kept by Hermann, Bishop of Constance, and nine others, who each narrate what they saw with their own eyes during a journey in the Rhine Provinces). He cured the sick, he healed the hurt. At his command the lame walked, the deaf heard and the blind saw. All kinds of diseases were banished with a touch or by a word, and the powers of nature seemed subject to his will. Sometimes the ludicrous blends with the supernatural; as when in the church of Foigny the saint cursed the swarms of black flies which were interrupting the service, and the offending insects fell dead on the floor; and the "*flies of Foigny*" passed into a proverb for centuries.

But I hear you say,—how do you explain all these so called miracles?—O unbelieving generation! How long will you doubt? The Talisman is FAITH! The witnesses to Saint Bernard's miracles were all earnest and sincere and truthful men, but they were also men of faith, and they had an inner and spiritual vision. And as modern science tells us that the eye can only see what it is prepared for seeing, so modern scepticism adds that what the eye is prepared for seeing it will infallibly behold! The miracles of the middle ages however, and of the Roman Catholic Church down to the present day, form far too wide a subject to be even glanced at now. It is closely connected with the modern phenomena of mesmerism, of catalepsy, of spiritualism and of trance.

★ ★ ★

I close by a sentence or two on the *character* of Saint Bernard.

"If ever there was a holy monk", said Luther, "it was Saint Bernard of Clairvaux"; and it is impossible to study his life without confirming the great reformer's verdict. Pious, beautifully pious, Bernard worships and adores with a seraph's love and with a seraph's fire! and he only changed his place and not his habit when he joined the angels' choir.

But in wondrous combination with his divine love was his matchless human energy, a force of will and of endurance almost beyond belief, and which held out, Promethean, to the end. He joined guileless simplicity with astutest policy; and his soul, like his eye, expressed the wisdom of the serpent and the harmlessness of the dove.

In a formal age, no one clung closer than he did to ceremony and ritual. But though tinctured with superstition, no one inspired the letter more fully with the quickening spirit. There is soul in all he does and in all he says.

By nature gentle and kind, he hated all tyranny but the tyranny of the church, for his gentleness was subjected mercilessly to his zeal. He would not tread willingly upon a worm, but he would burn men at the stake for attempting to explain the mystery of the Trinity.

He was as bold as a lion, and yet as modest as a violet. As ambitious as Caesar or Napoleon, as humble as Mary Magdalene.

Must it be added, I fear it must! that he did not, except indirectly, do much for humanity. He had no sympathy for advance or progress. He gave no aid to promote a pure theology or a true philosophy, or to emancipate mankind from their long thraldom. He lived in an age when new light was just beginning to stream upon the world, but he called on men to close their shutters and stir their fires. Bernard was a mystic, and the age was growing rational.

But I care not to dwell upon his faults and failings, which were rather of the time than of the man. I ask you rather to think of his gifts and of his graces; and so thinking, I trust you will not deem that you have mis-spent an hour midst the gloom of the Dark Ages with *Saint Bernard of Clairvaux*.

IV

SUBSTANCE.
A METAPHYSICAL THOUGHT

Delivered before the
Edinburgh Young Men's Christian Association
November 1878.

I always feel much difficulty in selecting the subject of an Introductory Lecture, and in combining the various and often somewhat inconsistent qualities which an opening address should possess, and in the present case my difficulty has been even greater than usual, from causes obvious enough.

On looking over the topics which are to form the

themes of your present series of Lectures, as well as those which have served as texts in former years, it has occurred to me that there is room for an Introductory Lecture of a *strictly metaphysical kind*, and indeed that some such lecture is almost imperatively demanded.

The mind requires, now and then, to get away from the clods and the fetters of earth and of sense, away into the empyrean, where the day is ever clear; and to drink, at its purest source, of the first good, first perfect and first fair. Now I take the opportunity of saying to you,—Young men, keenly desirous of mental and moral elevation,— Don't neglect Metaphysics! The Science of Mind, and the doctrine of the Unseen and the Universal! What are proudly though not quite justly called the *Physical Sciences* are perhaps now in the ascendant, (and very self-asserting some of them are); and there are not wanting among their votaries and champions those who arrogantly claim for them alone the name of "*Sciences*", as if the polar collocations and the whirling vortices of enchanted atoms were all that ultimately man could really know! There are some who say and think that they could find in the grey matter of the brain the very essence of the soul; and love and reverence and hope and faith and joy they call only the measured cadences of its tremulous vibrations. Now to such materialists, if any such there be, the proper answer is to be found in the truths and in the intuitions of ultimate metaphysics. Only go deep enough, and press analysis far enough, and the most obstinate materialist may be made to see that matter is not *all* the universe, and that there is something below and above and around and within it. Mind is not the outcome of trembling or rotating atoms. Neither qualities of matter nor thoughts of mind are self originated or self sustained. There are other spirits than volatile alcohols or irresolvable gases, and forces far more etherial and dominant than the expansion of steam or the explosion of gunpowder or of nitroglycerine; and vast as is the astonishing magnificence of the universe of suns and their mere material attendants, one soul outweighs them all!

★   ★   ★

It is and has always been one of the mischiefs and miseries of philosophy that almost all its words have been preoccupied by one or by many physical or material senses or significations, and they have to be purified by a new and regenerative baptism for the service of its mental and spiritual temple.

"Substance", according to its etymology, is derived from two Latin words, "*sub*" "under", and "*stans*" "stand–ing"; and it literally means that which *stands under* and supports anything. *Stans* has the force of subsisting, or permanently maintaining its position or office, and *sub* may mean in or within as well as under, and so we may paraphrase the word *substance* as signifying—"*That hidden reality which exists under the external appearance and qualities of anything, and to which all its appearances and all its qualities and attributes are to be ascribed.*"

This meaning of the word substance, which flows you see directly from its etymology, expresses generally its metaphysical or philosophical meaning. More shortly, "The *substance* of any thing is *that in which all its appearances, powers and qualities really subsist.*"

★   ★   ★

"Substance" has been one of the central words, and one of the central thoughts, in the discussions and in the controversies of Philosophy for more than two thousand years; and many, probably hundreds, of definitions of it have been attempted. Of course, it is out of the question to enter upon any examination of these; and most of them are so technical, that it would require a great deal of explanation, even to make their phraseology intelligible:—into this discussion, therefore, I cannot go to-night. But just to give you an idea of the matter, I will select as an example the definition given by one of the most eminent of the philosophers who have treated of substance;—I mean Benedictus de Spinoza;—and it will open perhaps a glimpse into the kind of disquisitions to which the subject leads.

Spinoza wrote in Latin, and some of you may like to hear the original words,—here they are. "Substantia est id quod in se est, et per se concipitur hoc est. Id, cujus conceptus non indiget conceptu alterius rei." "Substance is that which exists in and by itself alone, and which can be conceived only by itself; that is, the conception of which needs the conception of nothing else whatever."

★   ★   ★

The opposite or counterpart of Substance is called generally "*Form*"; and form and substance together make up the thing. Form means a great deal more than the mere shape or configuration of an object. It embraces all its outward and external qualities, and all its powers and attributes; in short, everything that makes the object what it is, everything by which it can be known or recognised; and Substance is the hidden bond which unites all these in *one*. And so, as you will easily imagine, *form* and *substance* together play an important part in the Scholastic disputations of the Philosophic ages.

Another pair of expressions nearly equivalent to Form and Substance, and which constantly recur in literature is "*appearance* and *essence*"; appearance corresponding to form and essence answering to substance, though the meaning is not quite equivalent. Here again, I need hardly say, "appearance" is not confined to the mere visual qualities of the thing,—qualities that can be seen,—but includes every attribute manifested by and proper to the object, whether it be corporal or mental, seen or unseen. *Essence* and *essential* and similar words have led to a world of endless controversy.

★   ★   ★

But now I beg leave to observe, and I pray you, Gentlemen, most emphatically to take notice, that we have got in this answer, and in the *substance* which we have now reached, new elements which are *not* material, I mean force and energy and motion. I entreat you, Gentleman, grasp these new elements firmly, particularly *force*, or *energy*, for I think motion is just a form of force, hold them fast and never let them go. We cannot do without them, the materialist cannot do without them. Neither can I! and I shall have need of them immediately again.

★   ★   ★

We have still very important steps to take in our search after absolute *substance*, I trust I may be permitted to assume without argument, especially in an association like this;—that the substance and essence of a man is his *reasonable* and *intelligent soul*. This is the cause and the explanation of all the phenomena which man presents.

★   ★   ★

And to come to the root and bottom of the matter at once,—I ask you to look at these *forces* and *energies* and *laws of nature* and *laws of life* and so on, which we have found as we went along to have so much to do with the phenomena we have been examining.

★   ★   ★

Do these forces and energies explain anything? Do they not just put the question farther back or farther on?—For the question is,—what is the substance of all the forces and energies themselves? They are not final and ultimate, they themselves need explanation, there must be something behind and beyond them. They are not self-originated, they are not self-maintained, they are but words telling us to go deeper and to go higher, and they all seem to say to the anxious enquirer,—"*not in us, not in us.*"

And now my friends, I think you are ready for our last upward step. The force behind and in all forces, the energy of all energies, the explanation of all explanations, the cause of all causes and of all effects, the soul that is within and below and behind each soul, the mind that inspires and animates and thinks in each mind, in one word the substance of all substances, the substance of all forms, of all phenomena, of all manifestations, is *God*.

"Nature! 'Tis but the name of an effect." The cause is *God*! Now we have reached a substance that does not in its turn become merely a form or phenomenon,—a substance which has nothing behind it, but of which all things past, present or future are but the *forms*.

Said I not that the word *substance* was perhaps the grandest word in any language? There can be none grander. It is the true name of *God*. Every line of thought meets here. Every eager question is answered here. Every difficulty and perplexity is resolved here. Here the philosopher must rest. Here the ignorant must repose.

Do you not feel with me that it is almost profane to

apply the word *Substance* to anything short of God? All lesser meanings are inadequate, all lower meanings are base. The universe and all its phenomena, suns and galaxies— with their inconceivable dependences, other universes, countlessly unthought, because unthinkable by finite minds, all,—all,—are but the forms of the Infinite, the shadows of the Substance that is One for ever.

★   ★   ★

It is mere repetition to say,—but it is not idle and vain repetition to say it, That if God be the *substance*, the *essence* of every force and of every being, He must be the very substance and essence of the *human soul*. The human soul is neither self-derived nor self-subsisting. It did not make itself. It cannot exist alone. It is but a manifestation, a phenomenon. It would vanish if it had not a substance, and its substance is God. Then it follows, infallibly follows,— but it is not needless to say it, God is the substance of your soul and of mine, aye, the very substance, its very self, in strictest truth. And your soul and mine are: but "forms" of God, (I am using the word in the scientific and strictly technical sense which I have explained), are but forms of God, dependent upon God the only "substance," for our momentary continuance.

And if God be the substance of our souls, He must also be the substance of our thoughts and of all our actions. Thoughts and actions are not self-sustaining and self-producing any more than worlds. They are mere manifestations first of our souls, but next and far more truly manifestations of God who is our ultimate Substance. "In Him we live and move and have our being." Observe the emphasis and the force of the *in*. "*In Him*." It is not said "by him" or "from him" or "through him" or "by his power." These may be all true, but not the truth declared here. It is *in* Him that we *have our being*. We are *parts* of the Infinite, literally, strictly, scientifically so. A human soul or a human thought outside of God would be a rival deity!

I pause here for a moment to remind you that I am not here to-night as a preacher, to teach theology, or even to teach religion, in the common sense of the word. I am here simply and solely as a scientific lecturer, trying to point out to you strict rigid scientific metaphysic and mental truth. I have not gone a single step out of my way as a student of metaphysic and mental science, and if I have had to speak to you of God, frankly and freely, that is only because God is necessarily found by all who fairly follow up the scientific idea of *substance* to its deepest roots and to its highest sources. The highest science always becomes religious,—nay, religion itself.

★   ★   ★

To resume,—and I think I shall make this my last observation, although the subject is inexhaustible. If God be the *substance* of all forces and powers and of all beings, then He must be the *only substance*, the only substance in the universe or in all possible universes. This is the grand truth on which the system of Spinoza is founded, and his whole works are simply drawing deductions therefrom.

"I am and there is none besides me,"—no being, no thing, no existence,—*I am*, and nothing else *is*.

If there could be two substances (and this idea of two substances is at the bottom of Dualism under all its names, it is found in a thousand forms in almost all religions); if anything else but God existed, anything outside God, anything of which God was not the substance,—then there would be two Gods, and *neither* of them would be *infinite*.

But I must forbear farther to trace the consequences of God being seen as the eternal and *only substance*. The subject may be expanded into many volumes. I think all of you must be satisfied by this time, that if this be a part of metaphysics, if this be only one chapter of metaphysics, these metaphysics can be no empty and barren science, but must be fraught with results and lessons as momentous as they are divine.

Take it not amiss if I add;—See to it that you be as humble as you are free. *Humanum est errare*. Error is natural, perhaps unavoidable to man,—but if we rest upon him, he who is our *Substance* will also be our *Guide*.

V

LAW A SCHOOLMASTER; OR, THE EDUCATIONAL FUNCTION OF JURISPRUDENCE

Introductory Address delivered before the Juridical Society,
Edinburgh, November 1878.

If the question were put, What is the great and leading purpose and end of Jurisprudence or Law in any state or nation? it would undoubtedly be a true and correct answer to say, The protection and security of life, liberty, and property among all the members of the community. And that law and that system of jurisprudence is the best which most perfectly accomplishes this object.

Every civilized community or state must select those rights and duties, the protection and enforcement of which it deems essential to the general wellbeing. It must *select*, I say; for it is not every right and every duty which can be enforced by law even in its most perfect form. An old Scottish lawyer quaintly said, "You cannot *poind* for charity," and so you cannot by any decree *ad factum praestandum*, or by any form of diligence, compel kindness, or consideration, or courtesy;—the highest duties are ever outside the region of earthly law.

Still there are some duties and some rights which may, in some good measure, and in a reasonable degree, be secured in observance and enjoyment by wisely framed laws; and each state will select for definition and enforcement (and the selection will constantly vary, according to circumstances) what it deems most essential for the commonweal. And this commonweal, or the greatest possible good and wellbeing of the community is and ought always to be the great end and object of every system of law. This is what may be called *law's chief end*.

★   ★   ★

Law is indeed an *educator*, a *teacher*, and the education which he gives is national, universal, and compulsory. In his ample schoolrooms there are places for all, and the pupil people, willing or unwilling, must learn his rigid lore, and what is more, they never fail to reach the standards of the appointed code. If the teaching is good and the standards high—if the law is just and right and noble—blessed be the people, assured of an onward and an upward course, ever nearing "perfection's sacred heights." But the converse holds also; and if the teaching of law is bad—if the national code is unjust and unrighteous, or low and degrading, so assuredly will the nation be; and under such tuition it will sink downward towards barbarism and blackness and death. Individuals may sometimes here and there rise above unjust and debasing laws; but never until the law be holy and its atmosphere be purged, never till then can the masses of the population breathe pure air, and either see or rejoice in the light of heaven.

*   *   *

And if any exigeant and inquisitive hearer presses me still further, and unreasonably demands that I shall exactly and precisely tell him what is this right which belongs to every man—what is this *"jus suum cuique tribuendum"*—this proper and peculiar and inalienable heritage of each man, which he may demand as of right, and which none may deny or withold; I am ready to meet this insatiable questioner also, and I say to him—adopting the definition of Herbert Spencer—that the *right* which belongs primarily, absolutely, and indefeasibly to every man, and of which no man can be deprived without outraging the laws of Heaven's Chancery, is "the right to exercise and enjoy to the fullest and to the uttermost *all the faculties* which God has given him, limited only by this, that he shall allow, and not interfere with or destroy, precisely the same liberty and enjoyment in every one else." I regard this as one of the best definitions of primary human right which has yet been framed. It admits, if applied accurately, of being wrought out to the uttermost, and of being successfully carried into the minutest particular of infinite detail. It is the technical embodiment and the scientific expression of the principle upon which rests the Divine precept, "Whatsoever therefore ye would that men should do to you, do ye even so to them;" "this is the law and the prophets." This is the root and foundation of that eternal equity or equality which rules over all, and which flows from the Divine nature itself. "O house of Israel, are not my ways equal? saith the Lord." And so, in a mysterious sense, it is said of the city of God, the perfection of holiness,—"The length and the breadth and the height of it are *equal.*"

★　　　★　　　★

Speaking generally, and without any attempt at strict scientific accuracy or precision, ethics or morality may be said to consist of three great regions or departments, which may be briefly characterized as embracing man's duty to his God, his duty to himself, and his duty to his neighbour. Now it is only the last of these three great divisions which, properly speaking, forms the province of jurisprudence or municipal law. Such law—municipal law—has only to do with man in society, with the rights and duties which arise to him as a social being, as a member of a community or a state. It is very important in many regards that this distinction should be kept clearly and prominently in sight. Jurisprudence—human municipal law—has no concern, directly and immediately, either with a man's duty to his God or with his duty to himself; and any attempted interference with either province for itself and for its own sake, and apart from society, is not only really impossible, and sure ultimately to be useless and abortive, but such interference is forbidden by the highest and most sacred principles of ethics and morality, and the contravention of these principles has in all ages been fraught with unmixed mischiefs and untold miseries.

★　　　★　　　★

In morality, as well as in science and in religion, the great mass of mankind are governed solely by authority. Even in relation to the most important doctrines of religion, doctrines involving not only temporal but eternal interests, the beliefs and the conduct of untold multitudes are governed and regulated simply and solely by what they have been told by those whom they accept as their authorized guides and directors, and whom they accept as such sometimes on the slenderest and the most infirm grounds. Do we not see in every country and in every nation that the religion of whole peoples and communities is determined by the mere accidents of their birth, or of the society among which their lot has been cast? They belong as a rule to what they call the Church of their fathers; and very often the best reason they can give for any faith that is in them is that it was their father's creed. I am not saying that this is wrong—probably it is inevitable. But I do say that it is a striking instance of how much the masses of mankind are prepared to accept, simply on what in a broad sense I call authority.

So it is with matters of science. Few indeed, very few, are either capable of verifying scientific truth or in circumstances enabling them to do so. The bulk of us must accept on trust what is told us through the recognised channels, and must passively receive the facts so given, and experience shows that we may safely do so.

Now, although morality is different from either religion or science, the case is exactly the same with it, though perhaps not to the same degree. The great bulk of men take their morality—their standards of right and wrong—from tradition, and from the authority of those among whom they live and move. It is vain to talk of morality being instinctive, and always and in all persons everywhere the same. This may be true of certain great moral truths which have been inwrought and practised for centuries, and which have become through many generations inborn parts of our nature, and common to the whole race. But the minuter details of morality vary in different countries and in different ages, and even in different extended societies and classes of men. Our moral sentiments, the accuracy and the vividness of our moral perceptions, and the certainty with which they act on our conduct, greatly depend on the moral atmosphere in which we live, and on the moral height and lucidity of the society which surrounds us; and this is what I mean when I say that the generality of men take their morality upon authority. They do and feel just as their reputable neighbours do, and they feel and conclude that what every one does cannot be wrong.

★   ★   ★

When at last a law is discovered by a few heaven-enlightened minds to be morally imperfect or morally wrong, how difficult it often is to break its thrall or procure its repeal or amendment! How the masses cling to it as good enough for them! How are the reformers stigmatized as utopian or visionary! The wisdom of our ancestors is declared to be better than the speculations of innovators, and the old landmarks are preferred to the new limits and definitions of an upstart system of ethics. Many a wrong has been perpetuated, not in the outward practice only, but in the hearts and minds and emotions of nations, simply because it has got consecrated by law.

★   ★   ★

There may possibly be suggested in some minds a difficulty, arising from the supposed inherent, eternal, and universal nature of moral truth. How can positive law of any kind, and however enforced, affect morality, which rests on a different basis altogether, which is written on the heart and the mind of man?

Now, to obviate this possible objection, it is enough to consider that it is not moral truth which is affected by jurisprudence or municipal positive law, but only *moral science*; not the truth itself, but only man's knowledge and perception of it. Moral truth, like every other kind of truth, is unchangeably and eternally the same. It is founded in the nature of *things*, as it is called—that is, in the nature of God. But moral *science*—that is, man's knowledge, man's *scientia* of morality—is constantly varying, now advancing, now receding; and moral science, like every other science, is essentially progressive, and capable of indefinite and infinite advancement. It is exactly the same with every other subject. The truths of astronomy or of mathematics or geometry are eternal and unchangeable. But the *sciences* of astronomy and of geometry are for ever imperfect and progressive, because they relate to the imperfect nature and the limited faculties of man. The very expression, "*the teaching of science,"* implies imperfect minds which are to be informed and enlightened by the teacher.

Now, the science or knowledge of morality is often in a very imperfect condition. Men do not *know*, except in a limited degree, what is true and just and right; and the thought—the single thought—which I present to you to-night is, that law is a most important and a most effective instrument for communicating and advancing that knowledge.

★   ★   ★

The great doctrines of *heredity* apply in their full force and vigour to *morality*. Moral qualities and moral habits are transmissible from father to son, and from generation to generation, and once rooted and fixed they become congenital and inherent in the race, and perennially flourish as the ages flow. Virtuous parents produce virtuous offspring. The children of the just are blessed. Is it not matter of thankfulness and rejoicing that in the case of every new individual—of every new child—we have not, so to speak, to begin at the beginning again. We have not the same rocks to blast and boulders to remove and weeds to eradicate—the soil comes to us prepared. The inheritance of holiness descends. The flying torch is passed from hand to hand and burns brighter as it runs. The great advancement of justice and of morality is not the labour of Sisyphus endlessly to be renewed, the results of the past are never lost. Each generation takes up the work where its predecessor left it, and adds to the rising pile, till, like a cathedral built by many generations, there soars to heaven the Temple of the Lord.

★   ★   ★

Legislators may often see the ideal right, but be unable to realize it. Parties and factions must be consulted and conciliated; obstructions must be soothed or softened; vested interests, though founded in venerable wrong, must be regarded and respected; and even omnipotent Parliament cannot always do the thing it would! Courts, too, are hampered by rule and form. Where the words of a statute are clear and unambiguous they must often disregard its injustice, and a *series rerum judicatarum* may often prevent the judgment which absolute equity requires. Where the words of a statute forbid, or where the point is absolutely ruled by precedent, it is vain to talk of equity to Lord Adam, or of eternal justice to the Justice-General!

But *you*, Gentlemen of the Juridical Society, are under no such fetters. Wherever right demands it, you may and you do condemn the statute, and review both the judgment and the judge. The decisions of the last resort are not final to you; and remembering that law must teach nothing that is not eternally true, you may always compare and correct its data by the handwriting that is on high.

In the spirit of this lofty freedom, I bid you God-speed in the session which you are now to begin. May the light of justice illumine all your discussions; may the love of justice burn in every heart; and, as the result of your meetings, may all of you experience that you are nearer the law and the love which is eternal and divine.

VI

THE TEN AVATARS OF VISHNU

Delivered before the Granton Literary Society March 1880.

There is an apostolic precept, the neglect or nonobservance of which, not only miserably narrows our minds and degrades us in selfishness, but wholly deprives us of the highest and purest pleasure of which our nature is suscept-ible. The precept is,—"Look not, every man on his own things, but every man also on the things of others." It is difficult, it is impossible, to say how much nobler and how much happier we should be if we constantly gave this precept our implicit obedience.

★   ★   ★

But the subject of my lecture to-night is only *one* of the doctrines of Hinduism, a doctrine which under many and varied forms has exercised a very marked influence on Hindu life and character, and which is full of lessons for ourselves. And it has, I think I may say, the deepest interest for every child of humanity.

This doctrine is generally known as

"*The Avatars of Vishnu*".

One or two sentences however must be given, to enable you to understand the position of Vishnu in the Hindu theogony, and the nature of his *avatârs*, or revelations, or incarnations.

Whatever Hinduism, or Brahmanism, may have latterly or in its bulk become, still in its purest and highest essence it was (indeed I think it still is, and I am glad to think so) a monism, a monotheism, and in one aspect a pantheism of a pure and noble kind. And as such it seems to me ever and again to reveal itself, not only in the early Vedic Hymns which are generally pointed to as its crystal sources of inspiration, but all through its voluminous sacred books,— all through its vast and unmanageable literature.

Pure Brahmanism knows only one God, indeed only one Being, in the universe,—"Brahm," or "Brahman," (neuter gender) in whom all things consist and exist, apparently for ever.

★   ★   ★

From this inconceivable and unnameable Brahm there issue—(*issue* is the word, and it is an eternal procession) the *Trinity* or *Triad* of the Hindus, with whom really begins their theology. The doctrine of a Trinity, though not the earliest, is one of the most prominent doctrines of Hinduism, and this itself is a very striking fact. The Hindu Trinity are these.

1. *Brahmâ*, the Creator, the Father.
2. *Vishnu*, the Preserver.
3. *Siva*, the Destroyer,

with whom is indissolubly connected the function of *reproduction*.

These are the Trinity, and all these are males. They have

names and they have gender, contrasting strikingly with the primeval neuter, the unutterable "Brahm!"

I have said that the Trinity issue from Brahm, and "issue" is the word, and the thought. Brahm does not create the Trinity. He is not creator and they are not his creatures. Perhaps "Manifestation" best conveys the idea. God is manifested in the Trinity! Three essences in one God! Three aspects of the Infinite!

★　　　★　　　★

Brahmâ, the First Person, is the Creator. He makes every person and every thing, from him all things took their origin.

But here his function stops, and it is very curious to observe how little original creation bulks in or impresses Hindu thought. Brahmâ, although he made all, called all into existence, is not figured as taking much interest in how the universe gets on, and so he has come to occupy quite a subordinate part in the actual worship and in the religious thought of Hindustan. Brahmâ is not with the Hindus as God the Father is with us,—the first or chief person in the Trinity. He is only first in order, not in importance. For every Hindu feels, as indeed we all should, if we were in his place, how far more important the preservation and the management and also the destruction and reproduction of the world and of its inhabitants are, than their mere original creation. It is everything to me how I am to be preserved and what is to become of me. It is very little to me how I came to be here at all. That is long past and a matter of small concern! Hence while there are many sects in India who devote themselves especially to the worship and service of Vishnu,—(*Vaishnavas* these sects are called), and perhaps still more who exalt especially Siva, the Destroyer and Reproducer,—(*Saivas*, and which last adore Siva's wife or female energy Devi), very few devote themselves to the worship of Brahmâ, whose work is thought of as done!

★　　　★　　　★

But I must hurry on to what I intended to be my sole subject, the Avatârs of the Second Person of the Trinity—the Avatârs of Vishnu.

An *avatâr* means in Sanskrit a descent, or coming down, but in the Vedas and in all the Sacred Books of Brahmanism it is almost exclusively applied to the descent of some deity to earth, either to avenge or to save. In Hindu theology it has this restricted meaning. As the descending god must take some form or other fitted for earth, and leaves, so to speak, his heavenly form behind, an *avatâr* has come to have very nearly the sense of the Christian word *incarnation*, and the Avatârs of Vishnu may be translated "Vishnu's Incarnations." Observe, however, that these incarnations must not be confined to the human form, human flesh. An avatâr may be in any form whatever.

All the Hindu deities from time to time make avatârs, some of them many thousands or millions of times, and in every conceivable form and circumstance. To-night we confine ourselves to the best known descents or incarnations of Vishnu.

In all religions incarnations are known. Ever and again man's spirit tells him,—"The gods are come down to us in the likeness of men." In the crowd or in the solitude, by night or by day, ever still the heavens are opened, the dazzling smites us to the ground, and "deep calleth unto deep." Whence this inextinguishable belief? From the felt possibility, nay the certain truth, that the Infinite can come down, has come down, and is manifest upon earth. Where is the soul so dead and so lost as not to have had its avatâr, and not often to await the visitor from on high? Vishnu in Brahminical mythology is the Preserver, and has often come down, made a descent, an avatâr, to vindicate and to save.

★   ★   ★

The Ninth Avatâr, the last which has yet taken place, is quite distinct in character from all the others, and stands alone and unique. It is the *Buddha* Avatâr, the incarnation of *Vishnu* as *Buddha*.

Buddha was the great reformer and preacher, of kingly race, who arose in Hindustan about six hundred years before Christ, and was the founder of that mighty religion which is called *Buddhism*, and which in many respects was a revolt against *Hinduism*, particularly as to caste, the origin of the gods, and the destiny of man.

In primary or original theology, in speculative theism, and in the grand doctrine of the Immanence of God, I think that Buddhism is far inferior to Brahmanism, but it is greatly superior in its moral teaching, and indeed the wonder is that moral teaching so high should be rested on a system which it is difficult to defend from the charge of being atheistic. But the only point with which we are concerned is, that, after Buddhism had made some progress, Hinduism, instead of denouncing it as a rival, did not hesitate to adopt its founder as a Deity and to admit him into its Pantheon. Buddha was welcomed as an Incarnation of Vishnu. This opens a wide field for speculation, as interesting as it is forbidden to us to-night. Truly Hinduism may claim to be a *catholic* religion.

This ends the past Avatârs. But Brahmanism has a future too! God's revelations are not over, are not completed. We have not yet heard His last word, we shall never do so. We look for His *coming* still, and hymns like the Christian's are also sung in Hindustan.

★   ★   ★

There even now approaches the tenth Avatâr which our Indian brethren call the *Kalki*, the more than millennium of blessing, when the law and all the ceremonies of the Vedas shall cease, when without law each shall be a law unto himself, "perfect as the Father in Heaven is perfect." In these hopes and aspirations of the Hindu may not the Christian join? and whatever names or languages we use may we not unite in the wish, which is the prayer, "Thy kingdom come!"

I have left myself and you no time to draw any lessons, or even to indicate the many and very grand deductions which flow from the Indian doctrine of the *Ten Avatârs*. Perhaps it is better so. Better that I should be silent. Silence is sometimes the most impressive teaching. *Think* on these things!—And so, without attempting to read a single lesson, or to draw a single deduction, I close this imperfect and hasty lecture by making a supposition which I daresay has occurred to many of you as we went along.

Suppose an educated Hindu, without abandoning his own faith, to study, as many cultivated Hindus most eagerly do, the principles and the doctrines of Christianity.

Might we not expect to hear him say, not with surprise but with glad sympathy;

> "I find many beautiful analogies between this Western faith and the vaster creed of my country and my youth. Here too, as in the plains of India, the gods dwell with and in men. Christians too have their Avatârs, and I find the great central doctrine of Christianity, that on which all its other doctrines turn and revolve as on a pivot, to be an impressive, most mighty, and most magnificent Avatâr;— God manifest in the Flesh!"

VII

THE TWO FOUNTAINS OF JURISPRUDENCE

Delivered before the Scots Law Society, Edinburgh
November 1880.

It is forty years ago (I think upwards of forty years ago) since I joined the Society as an ordinary member. For a good many years I took an active part in its debates, and in its business of every kind. I believe I was duly found maintaining the affirmative or the negative both of legal and of speculative questions, as the Secretary or the Case-book ordered me; I gave opinions which I thought were sound, and wrote essays which I thought were instructive; I found many friends, in concert or in conflict with whom I learned both respect for the opinions of others, and courage and confidence to maintain my own; and when, after attaining what was called then "honorary privileges," I ceased to attend your Hall and left the arena to fresher and younger spirits, I did so with a grateful consciousness, which I still feel, that to the Scots Law Society I owed not only many happy evenings and many pleasant recollections, but also many lasting and substantial mental benefits. It had made me a better informed, a better equipped, a more skilful, a more ready, and at the same time a more modest and an humbler man than I had been before.

★   ★   ★

There are two, and only two, ultimate fountains of jurisprudence; namely *Morality* and *Policy*.

★   ★   ★

I have always thought it one of the advantages of a society like this, that it was entitled, if not bound, in all its discussions, to be perfectly free and absolutely speculative. To be speculative, not only in its properly speculative questions, but also in its legal ones. It is always entitled to ask, not only what the law *is*, but also, and often chiefly, what it *ought* to be. This is a privilege which is not conceded to other tribunals than such as yours.

Now I want you to use this privilege freely and boldly. I myself claim my share of it for this short hour, (alas, I shall lose it soon!) and casting away, while my dream of liberty lasts, the statute book and the libraries of decisions and every rag and remnant of usage and of authority, I go with you, in the freshness of creation, to trace and to test every law as in the light of its earliest morning when its history is all to make.

And it is good for us all to do this now and then. Back to first principles, when the logic is long and the links are twisted! Down, down to the foundations, when the turrets are tottering and the ridges reel,—and feel how firm these foundations are, on the moveless yet living rock! And think not that it is mere useless trifling, thus to go back and thus to go down. Practical results will surely and ultimately follow. If first principles have not been truly carried out, if on the firm foundations the walls have not risen rightly, by truest plummet perpendicular towards heaven, and by bedded block parallel to the horizon; then, be sure, that sooner or later we must begin again, for Nature will find out our failure, and with her there is no forgiveness.

★   ★   ★

The proposition which I am submitting to you, as to the foundations of Jurisprudence, is not a historical proposition at all. I do not think of it in a historical light, and I do not mean to trace it in historical manifestation or illustration. I look at it rather, and only, in a philosophical or scientific aspect; and without intending at present to enquire into its action and influence in remote times, or amidst savage surroundings, I say that *now* and for actually existing communities, for you, and for me, and for all existing governments, the law that is not well and securely founded either on true and eternal morality, or on wise and just and beneficent expediency, that law, however venerable it may be in its antiquity, with whatever fair and favored associations it may be entwined, and whatever interests may have grown up around it, should be abrogated and blotted out, as a groundless and unwarrantable interference with the freedom and the spontaneity of man.

And so, you see, our thought, harmlessly speculative as it may at first sight appear, may easily, and as it were in a moment, become destructively radical; and the thinkers, by the very might and majesty of their thoughts, and by the clearness and by the cogency of their speculations, be driven into action with a might and a momentum that is irresistible!

I assume in this argument, what is abundantly clear, and what is demonstrated and evolved and illustrated from more than one chair in this University; that there is an eternal and unchangeable system and scheme of morality and ethics, founded not on the will, or on the devices, or in the ingenuity, of man, but on the nature and essence of the unchangeable God.

★   ★   ★

It may be a question, and it has been the subject of endless controversy, in what does this eternal and unchangeable rule of rectitude consist and subsist, and there are many conflicting theories as to the essence and ground of changeless morality.

★   ★   ★

The contest is not as to the reality and meaning of eternal ethic, but as to whence cometh its mighty power. Admitting, as all do, the prowess of this Sampson, the only question which remains is, wherein his great strength lies, that we may understand it better and rejoice in it more!

Are morals intuitive? Is there a moral sense within us, which pronounces at once upon what is right and wrong, as do our eternal senses upon what is hard or heavy or bright or scarlet or loud or bitter or sweet? Do morals rest upon the will of God? or do they go deeper than his will and repose for ever upon his eternal nature? Which system shall we adopt, by which shall we classify phenomena that are unchallengeable? The selfish system, which tells us that every thing that is brightest and best is but enlightened and far-seeing self-love? The sympathetic system, which boldly substitutes altruistic for egoistic idealism? The utilitarian system, which traces all good to the production of the ultimate happiness of the many or of the all? Or any other of the mixed and intermediate theories which seek to explain the *"beauty of holiness"*?

I ask not what view you take among these rival and perplexing pretensions, so only you be sure of this, that there is an eternal and an unalterable morality, which is as pure as God and as immovable as is his throne! And if you grant me this, (as who does not?) then I say that the first requisite of every earthly law, I care not on what subject, is that it shall conform, implicitly, and down to its minutest jot and tittle, to the law that is written in heaven.

★   ★   ★

The first question as to any law, or as to any legal proposition, is and must always be,—Is it just? Is it right? Is it in conformity with the canons of Heaven's Chancery, rounded as the spheres, and straight as the rays which issue from the throne of God?

When you have got this question answered, this first question,—Is the law or proposition just? is it right? is it equal? is it equitable?—then and not till then, may you freely proceed to the other questions, and ask how such points have been decided, and what have great judges or great jurists thought about them.

It is a bad way to begin *your* legal discussions, it is a bad way to use *your* speculative freedom, to begin by saying, "This question was virtually but conclusively decided in the first Division or in the second Division or in the House of Lords in the case of John Doe against Richard Roe, and here are the words of the Lord Justice General, or of the Lord Justice Clerk,—or of the greatest Chancellor who ever pressed the woolsack!"

★   ★   ★

The faculty of seeing and knowing the right and the just is a progressive faculty, and its growth is slow and feeble. Our moral judgments are not the same as those of our ancestors. What seemed just to the last generation is no longer just to this one. The justice of to day is less perfect than that of to-morrow! The moral sense, as it is called, is constantly being corrected by the opening and increasing intelligence;—as we know more, we see better; and as we trace cause and effect from link to link and from chain to chain, and see from afar what mighty results arise from slight divergences and from seemingly indifferent beginnings, the moral sense seems to lay down its functions and asks to be led by the cultured intellect, to which is slowly being revealed the hidden causes wonder-working for ever "in the process of the suns."

And so morality is not a fixed, but a growing science; and it is not an independent, but a dependent and superadded science! It is superior to, and yet dependent upon, all the discoveries of intellect and of science, of history and of metaphysic. It can judge with authority, but others must bring to it the materials for judgment, and with every addition and new importation of these materials the cause must be reheard and the judgment reviewed, and the decision may be different at every trial!

★   ★   ★

The law always lags behind ethical science, but always tries to keep it in sight, and often somewhat ludicrously limps lamely after it. I say after ethical science, not after absolute justice or equity. Absolute justice, absolute equity is always the same,—perfect as God is. But ethical science is Man's knowledge of that divine law, which knowledge is always varying, and always partial and imperfect,—but let us hope constantly improving and increasing.

★   ★   ★

I have said enough, I doubt not, to suggest to you (for you are not new to these themes) the relation of ethics and their paramount importance as the great and the primary fountain of law, from which must ever flow all its streams and all its streamlets, and to which they must ever owe all their purity and all their sanitary power.

And I hasten on to consider what I have ventured to name the other fountain of jurisprudence,—*Policy*.

★   ★   ★

Considerations of policy, regard being had to far distant and widely operating effects, are quite as important,—sometimes they are even more important,—than even considerations of present equity; and so I feel disposed, in view of ultimate consequences, to place the two fountains, the two foundations of Jurisprudence, almost in equal rank,—the rightness of both being almost equally necessary for the welfare of a nation. I shall remark immediately, and give the reason why, this almost equal ranking of policy with equity is not inconsistent with the paramount allegiance which is due to immutable morality. In ultimate analysis, the two are one.

★   ★   ★

It will be well spent time,—to dwell upon, to trace, and to discover the principles of ethics, before you commit yourselves to the guidance of alleged principles of positive law. Descending from moral heights, you will find you have been upon a vantage ground, from which you have got a commanding survey of the lower fields of earthly law, and your pleading robes in the Courts of Jurisprudence will shine with light from the Mount of Transfiguration! You will cast your arguments in quite another shape, as to the meaning of a statute or the construction of a deed, after you have been in a region where the statutes are all divine and the covenants only righteousness; and the light that guided you among the ordinances of Heaven will not be found unavailing when you have to thread your way and pick your footsteps in the darker regions of earthly law.

★   ★   ★

To those who rightly estimate the value and importance of tracing the spring and source of law, the history of its progress as it flows onward from its source is deeply and profoundly interesting. For the stream always tells of its source. All the variations which are found in different nations and in different ages, throw light backwards upon moral science. The laws of a people are veritable history, incapable of being falsified or forged, and nowhere is the advance and improvement of ethics more clearly read than in the progressive history of the world's laws. And we find there too the prophecy of the future, onward and for ever on, new knowledge softening the severity and correcting the mistakes of law, widening man's freedom while drawing closer his brotherhood, till at last love is liberty and nature law.

This result societies like yours powerfully advance. Night by night, at every one of your meetings, some old prejudice gives way; some new view is got of the perfect and the fair; some successful attempt is made to put actual law in accordance with the ideal; some popular fallacy is detected and exposed and exploded; and so, in a thousand ways, the work goes on, till by little and little the kingdom is won!